The Artwork of 3ichael 7ambert
Volume V

By

Michael Andrew Lambert Jr

Prologue

Welcome to "The Artwork of 3ichael 7ambert: Volume V," a thoughtfully curated showcase of my artistic journey. This book serves as a glimpse into my creative universe, highlighting the variety of mediums and styles that have shaped my work throughout the years. From detailed drawings and vibrant paintings to groundbreaking multimedia creations, each piece conveys a story, captures a fleeting moment, or delves into a concept that holds personal significance for me.

My artistic inspiration stems from a mix of intuition, creativity, and a passion for problem-solving. Through my art, I strive to stir emotions, provoke thought, and forge a deeper connection with my audience. Whether you find yourself captivated by the intricate details of a sketch, the striking brushwork of a painting, or the layered complexity of a multimedia work, I hope each page encourages you to see the world from my perspective.

Thank you for taking the time to delve into this collection. I invite you to accompany me on this journey through the development of my artistic voice, and I sincerely hope my creations resonate with you as profoundly as they do with me.

Dedication

This book is a tribute to the amazing peers, teachers, and mentors who have influenced my artistic journey.

I want to express my gratitude to my Art Teachers at Rangeview High School, Kyle Riggins and Jennifer Minor. Your support and encouragement have allowed my creativity to flourish and have inspired me to delve into the depths of my imagination. The foundation you provided has been essential to my love for the arts.

To my mentor at Rocky Mountain College of Art and Design, your guidance and perspective have been crucial in my development as an artist. Your faith in my abilities has motivated me to challenge myself and keep growing.

Thank you all for being integral to my artistic journey. This collection embodies the knowledge, inspiration, and support you have shared with me.

Artist Statement

I am a multimedia artist who views art as more than mere creative expression; it's a lifestyle. To me, art goes beyond traditional boundaries, manifesting in every facet of life. Whether I'm painting, drawing, working with digital media, or sculpting, my creations reflect the belief that creativity knows no limits and is always present.

In my artistic journey, I experiment with a variety of materials and techniques, never limiting myself to a single form or style. Each artwork I produce is a testament to my conviction that art is omnipresent, just waiting to be uncovered and shaped. My process is both intuitive and experimental, allowing the journey to inform me as much as the initial idea.

For me, art transcends mere visual appeal; it's about living genuinely, appreciating the beauty in everyday experiences, and discovering inspiration in the unexpected. My creations invite others to view the world through this perspective, encouraging them to recognize the artistry in their own lives and to connect with the creativity that surrounds us.

Through my work, I strive to dissolve the lines between various mediums and disciplines, creating a rich tapestry of experiences, emotions, and concepts. My aim is not only to produce visually striking pieces but also to motivate others to embrace an artistic lifestyle, seeing the potential for art in all their endeavors.

In this sense, my art serves not just as a reflection of my creative vision but as a call to integrate art into the very fabric of life—a journey that encompasses both creation and discovery.

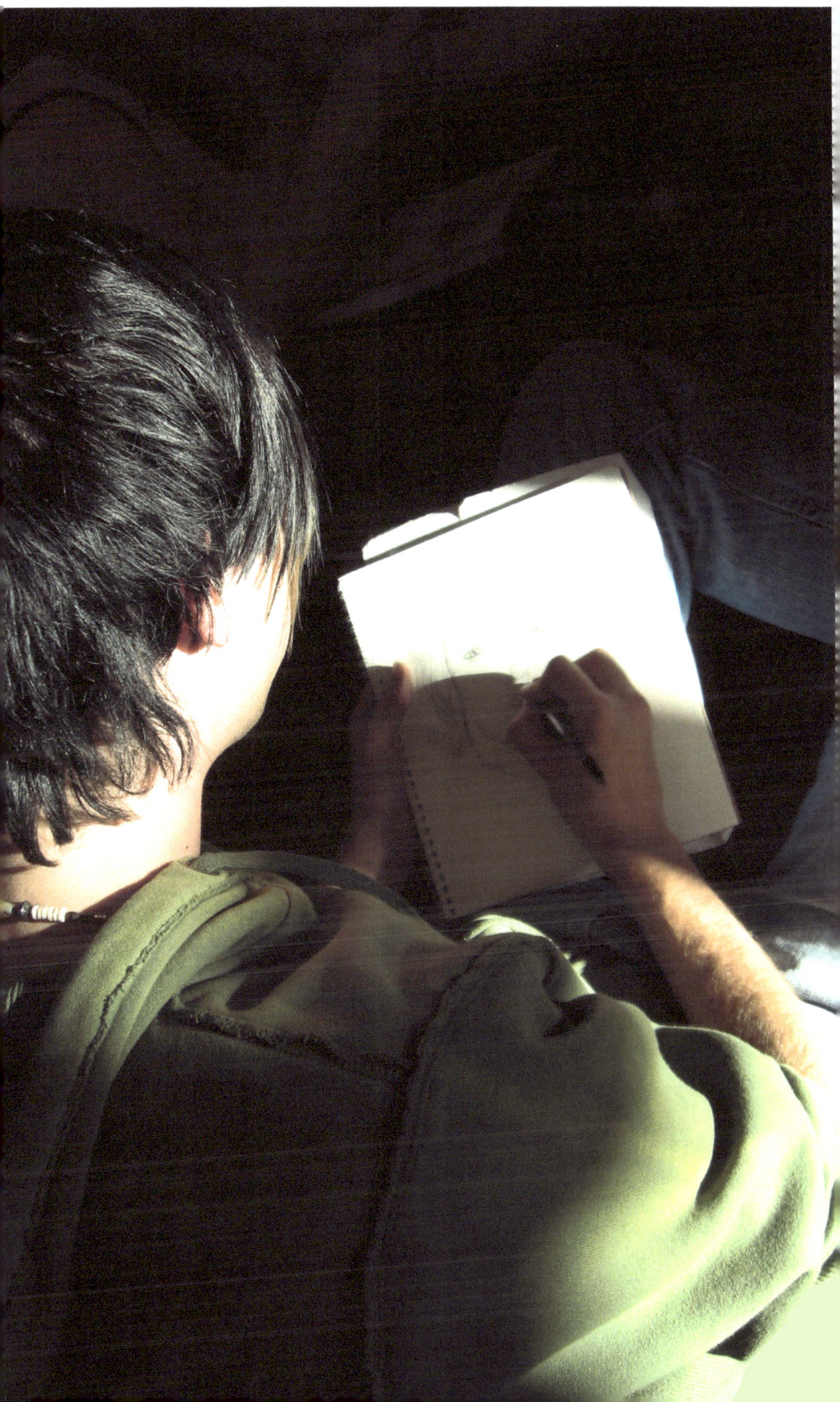

"Paint Girl"
2021
Digital

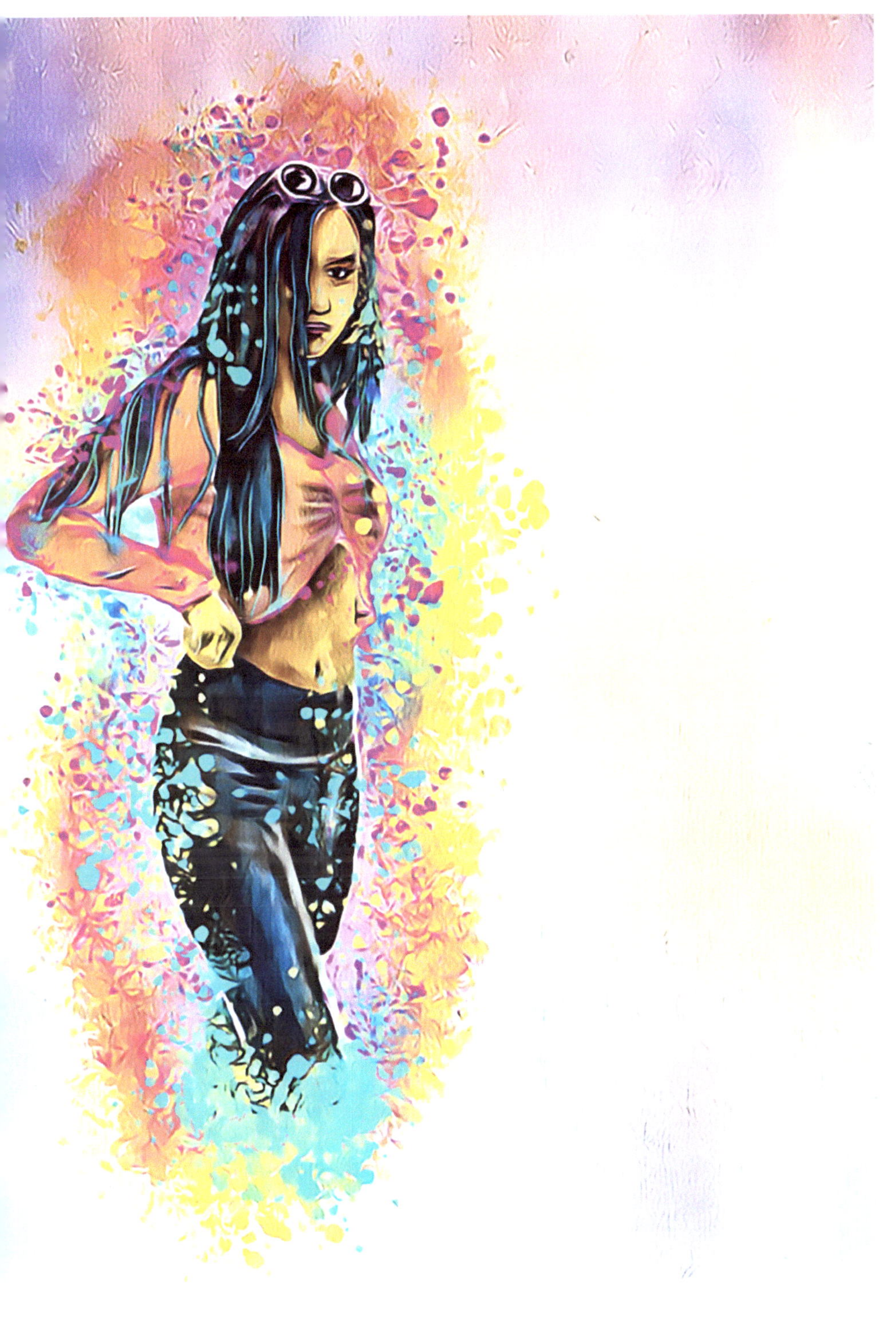

"Jellyfish"
2021
Digital

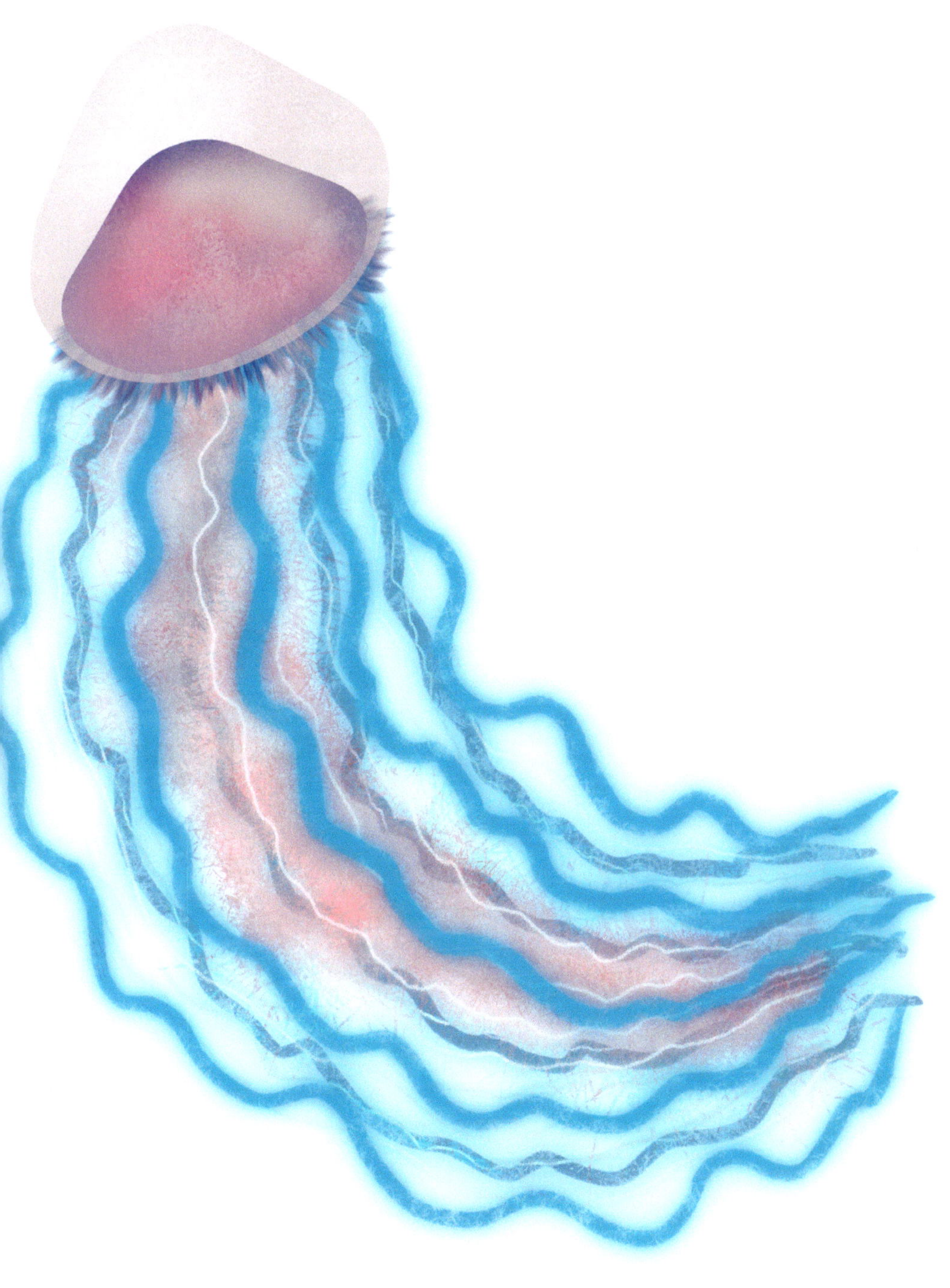

"Jellyfishes"
2021
Digital

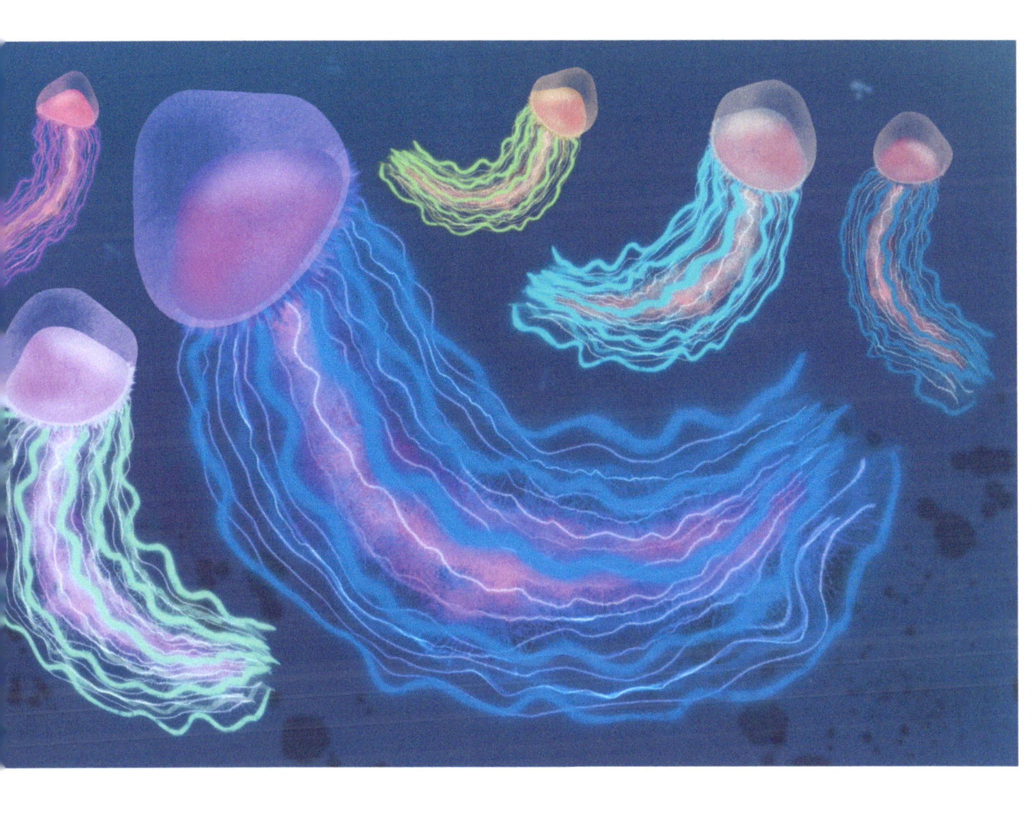

"One Star Dragoball"
2020
Digital

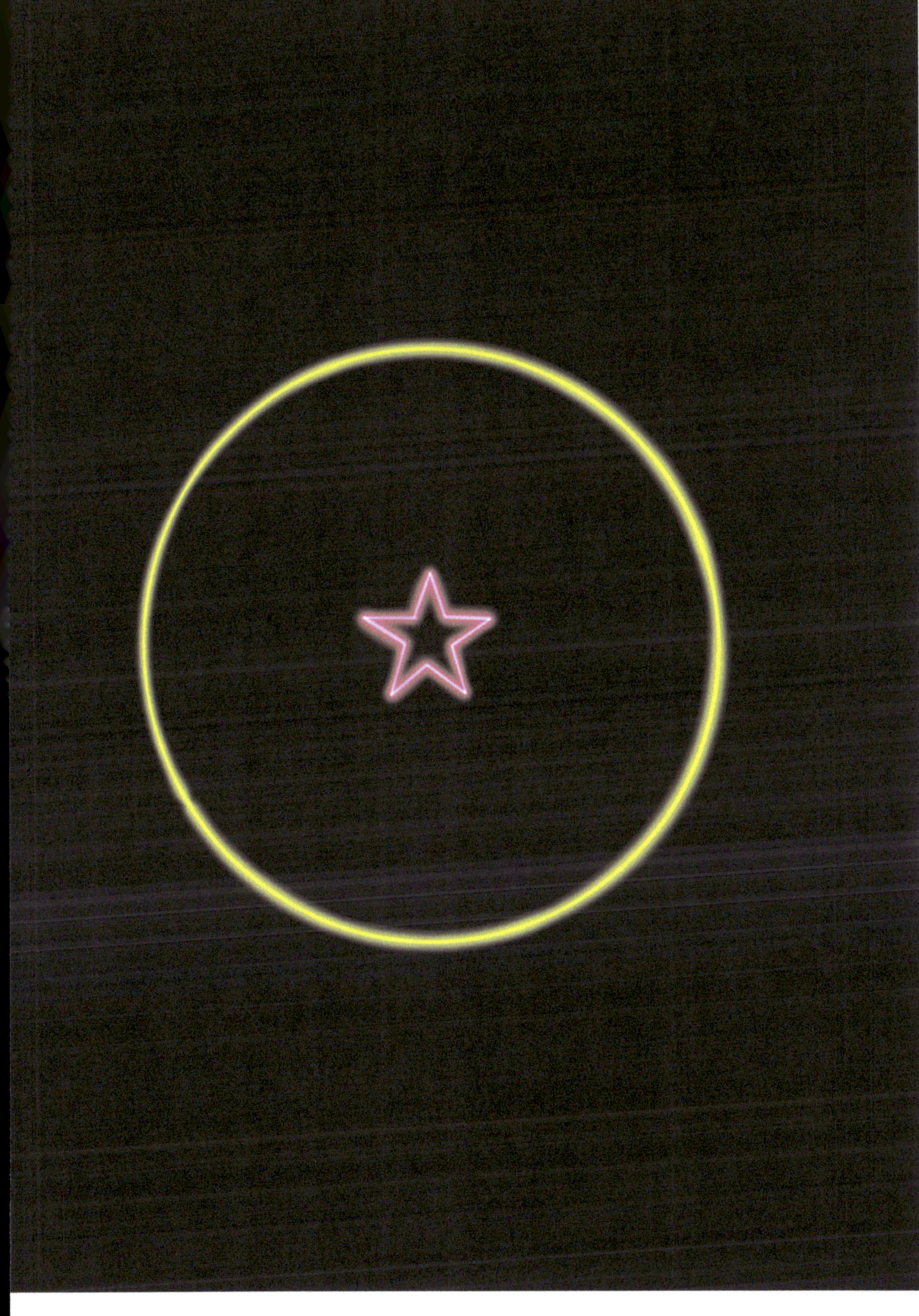

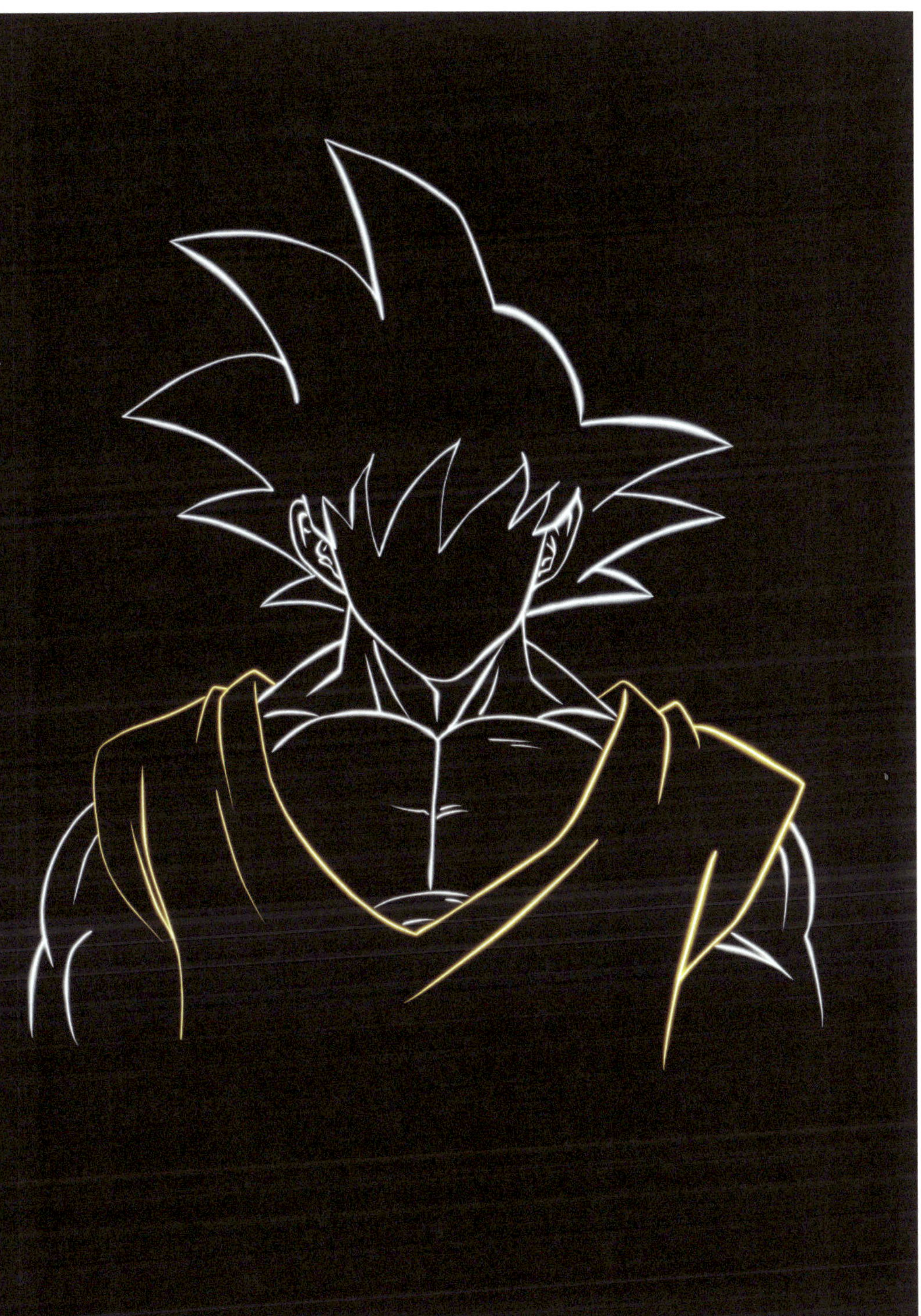

"Japan"
2021
Digital

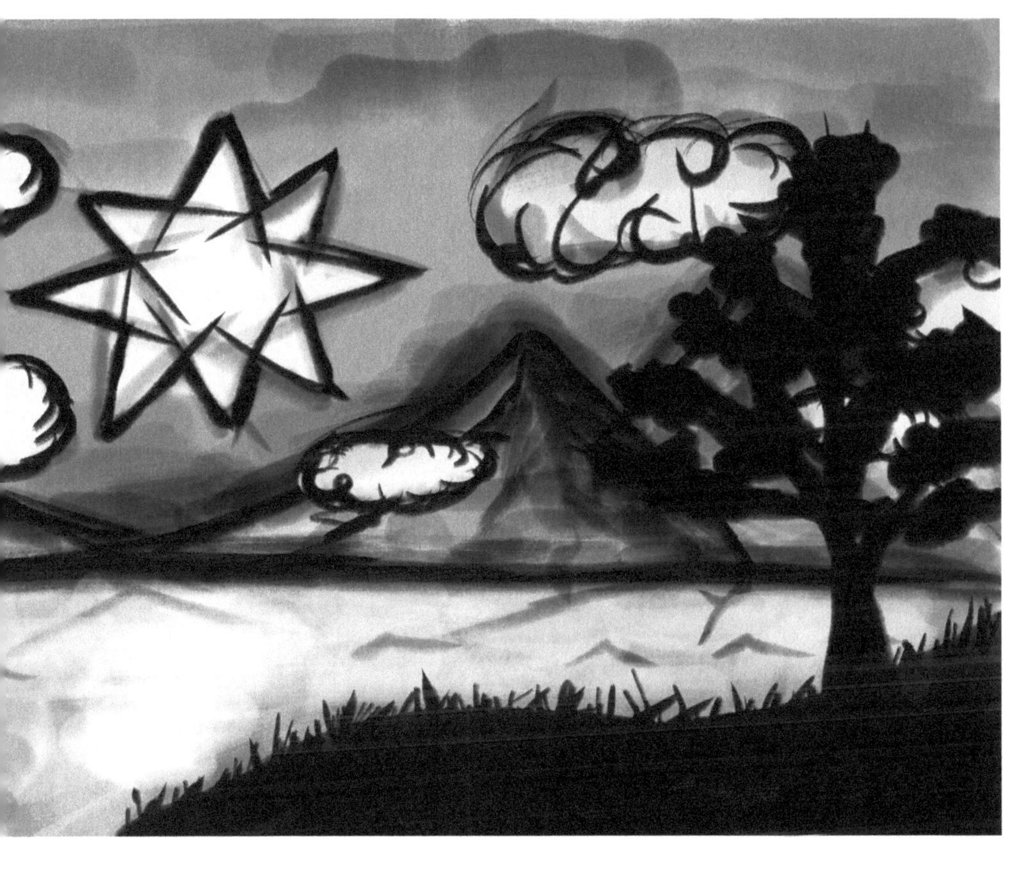

"Bunny Bulma"
2021
Digital

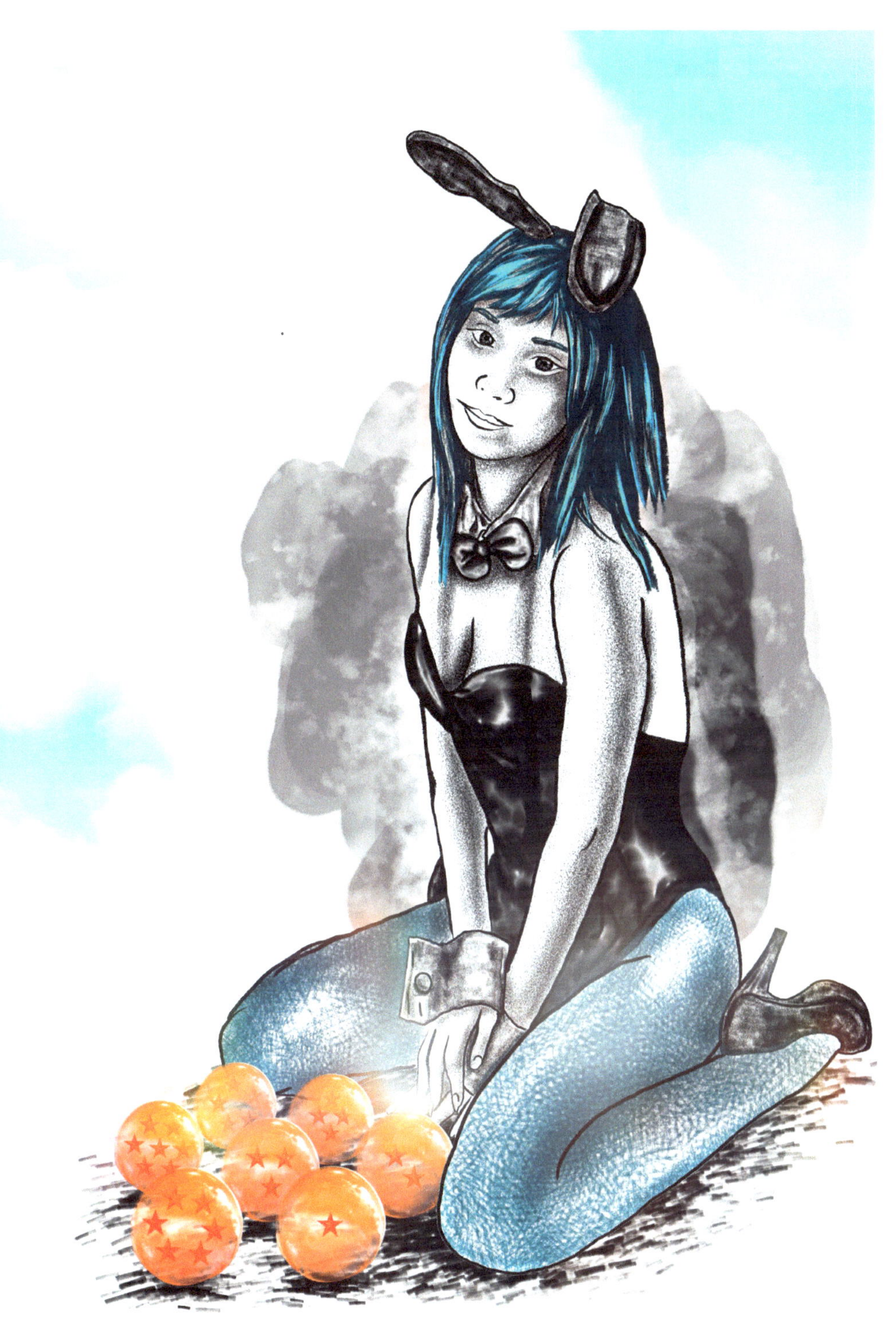

"Depths"
2020
Digital

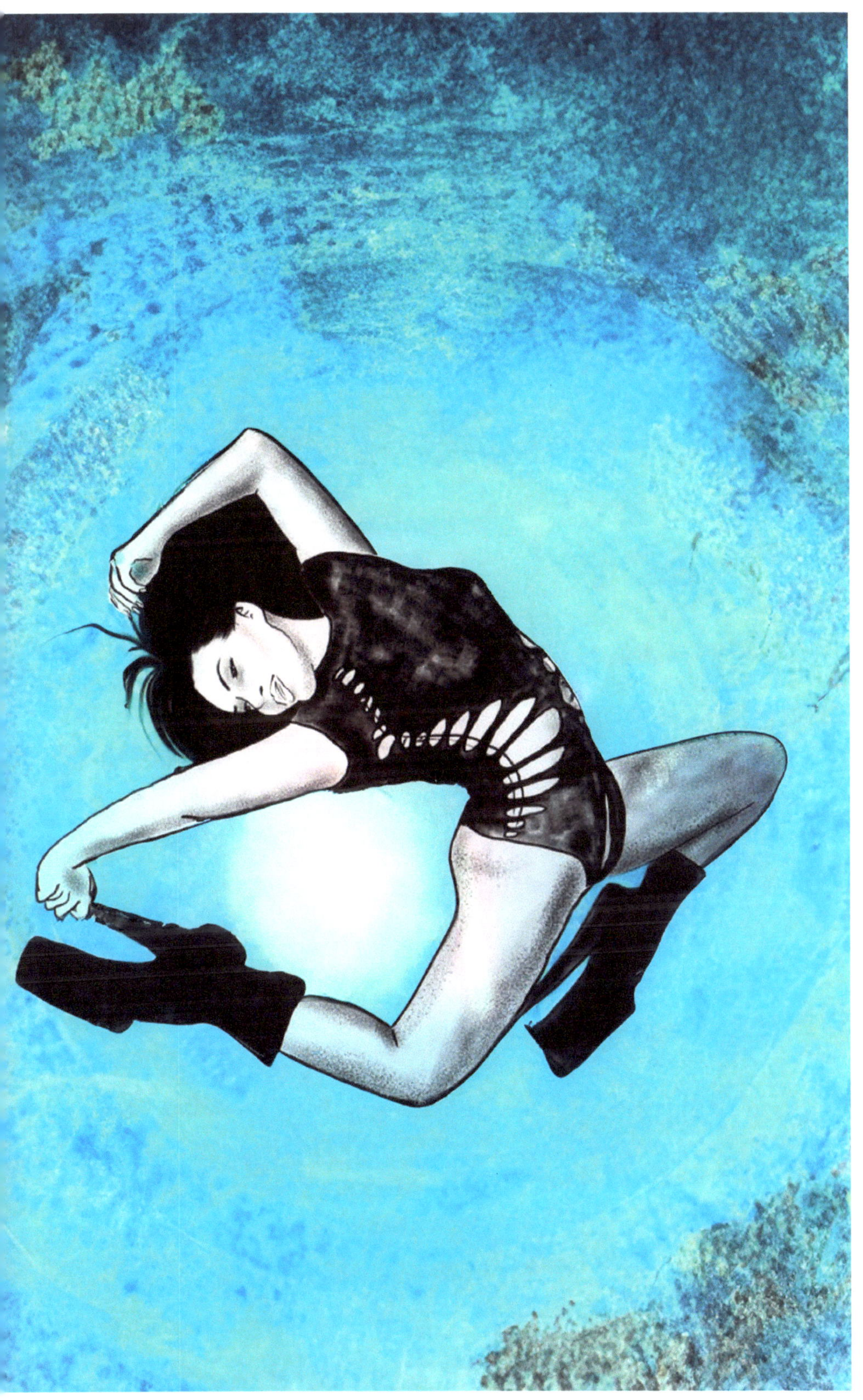

"Cherries"
2019
Digital

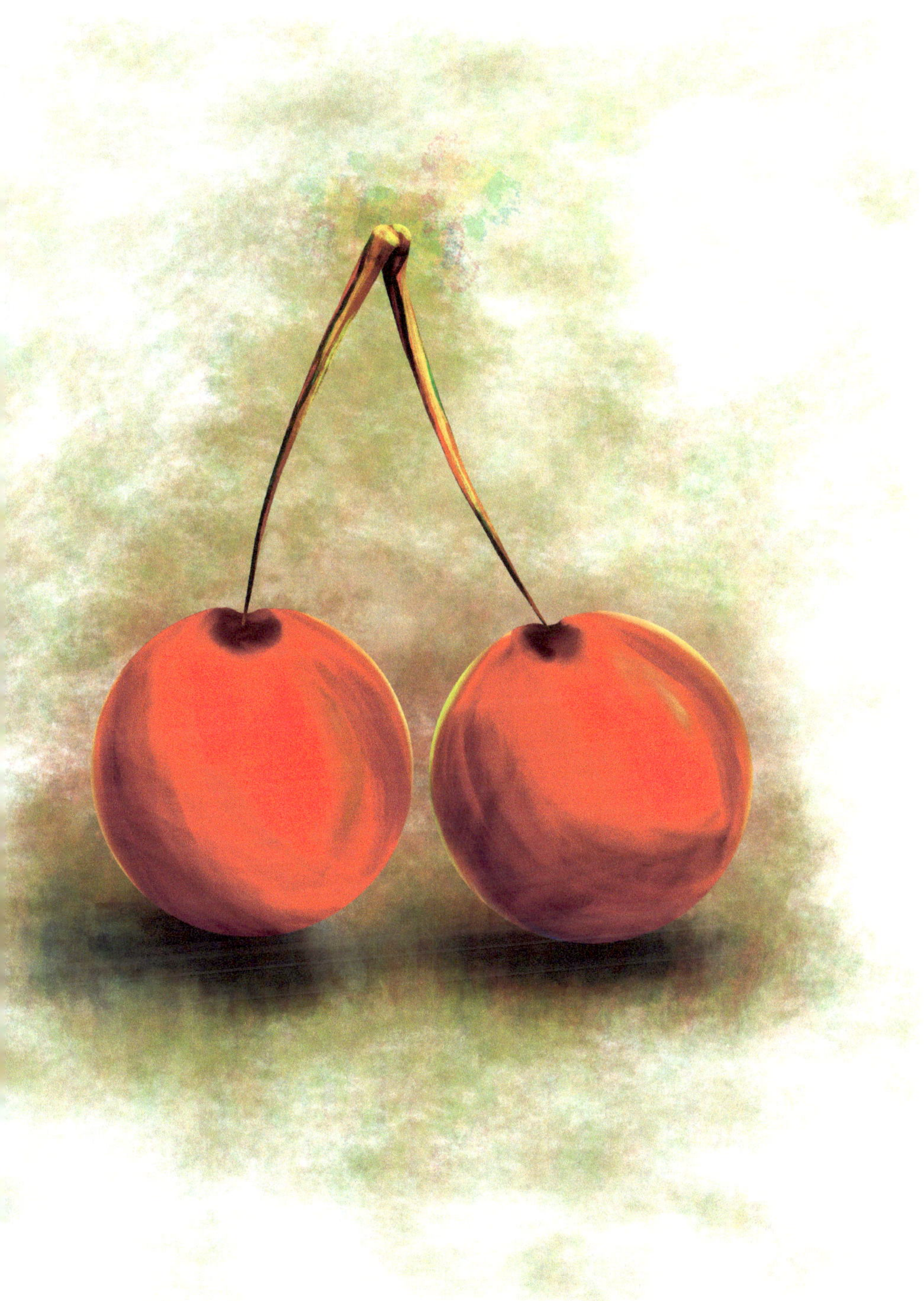

"Mouse"
2018
Photography

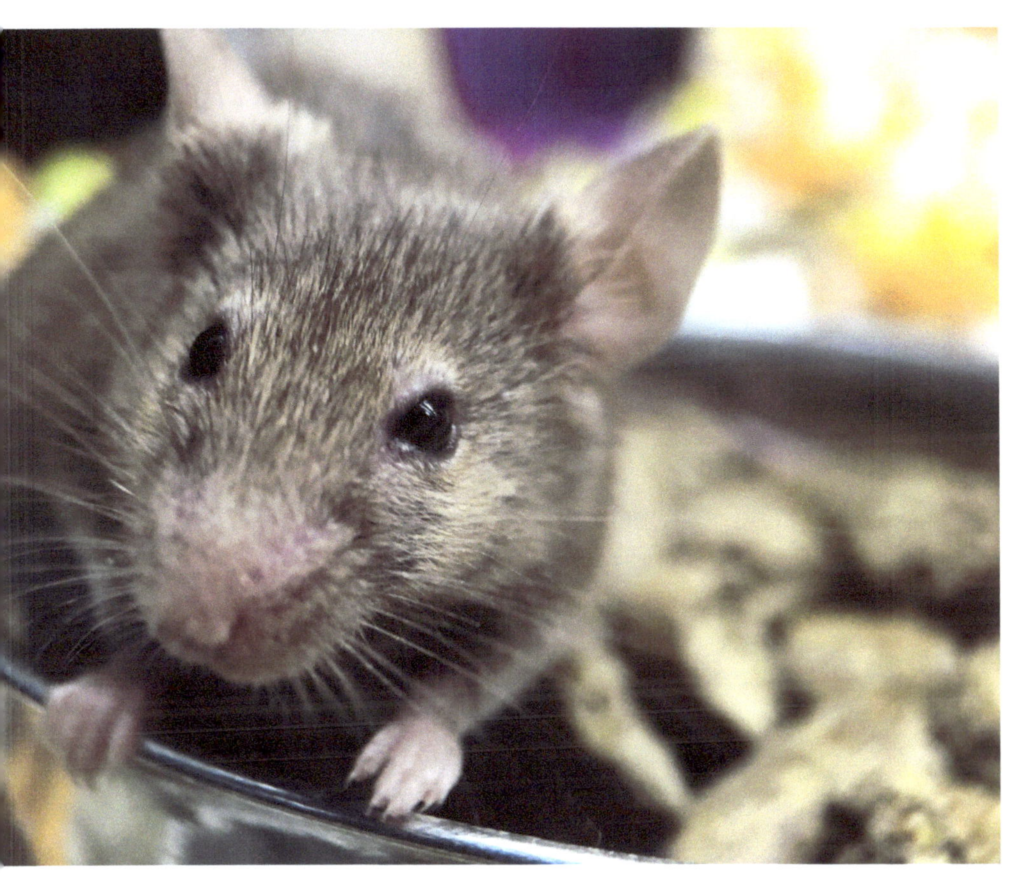

"Urban Girl #Pink"
2020
Digital

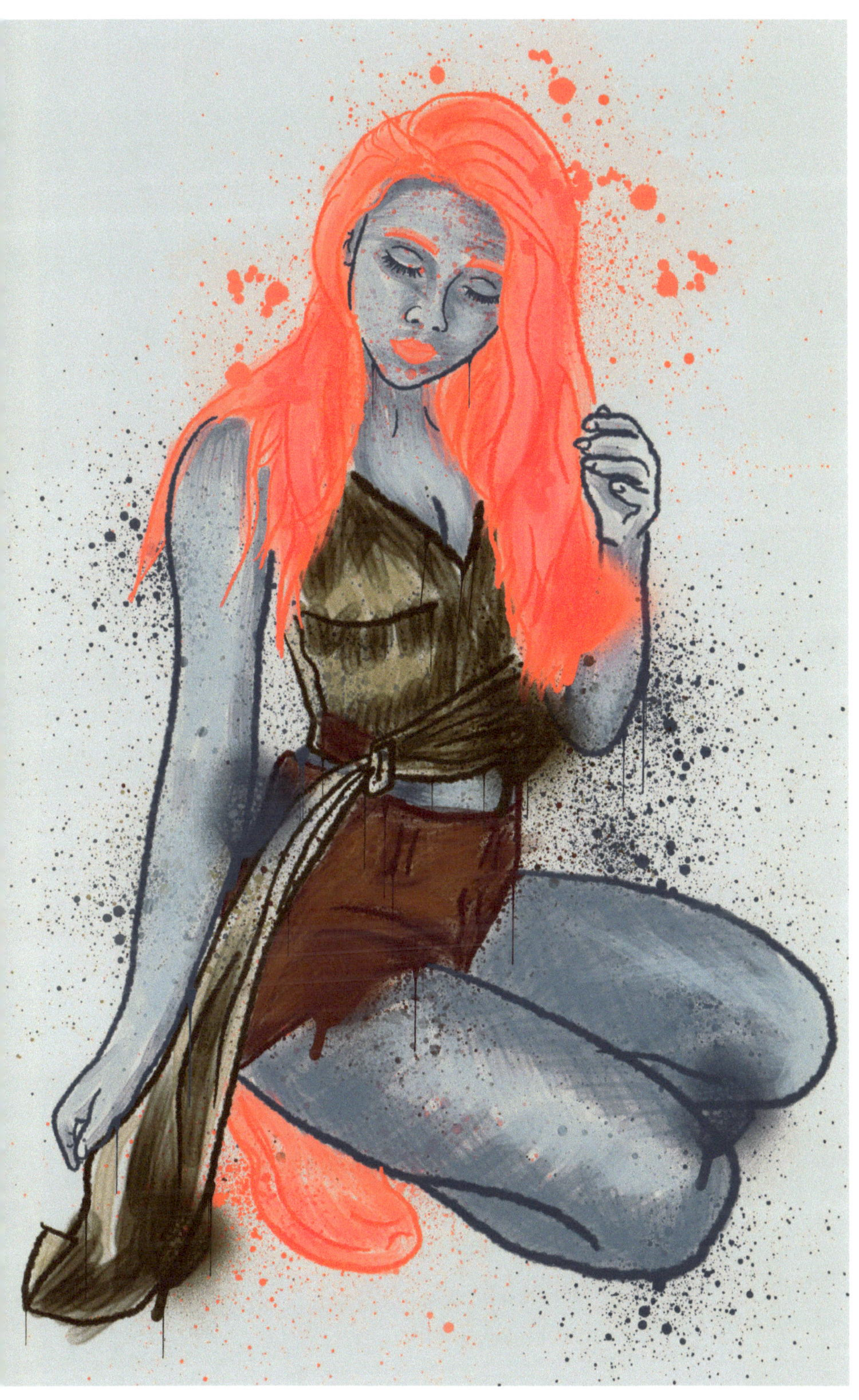

"Urban Girl #Brown"
2020
Digital

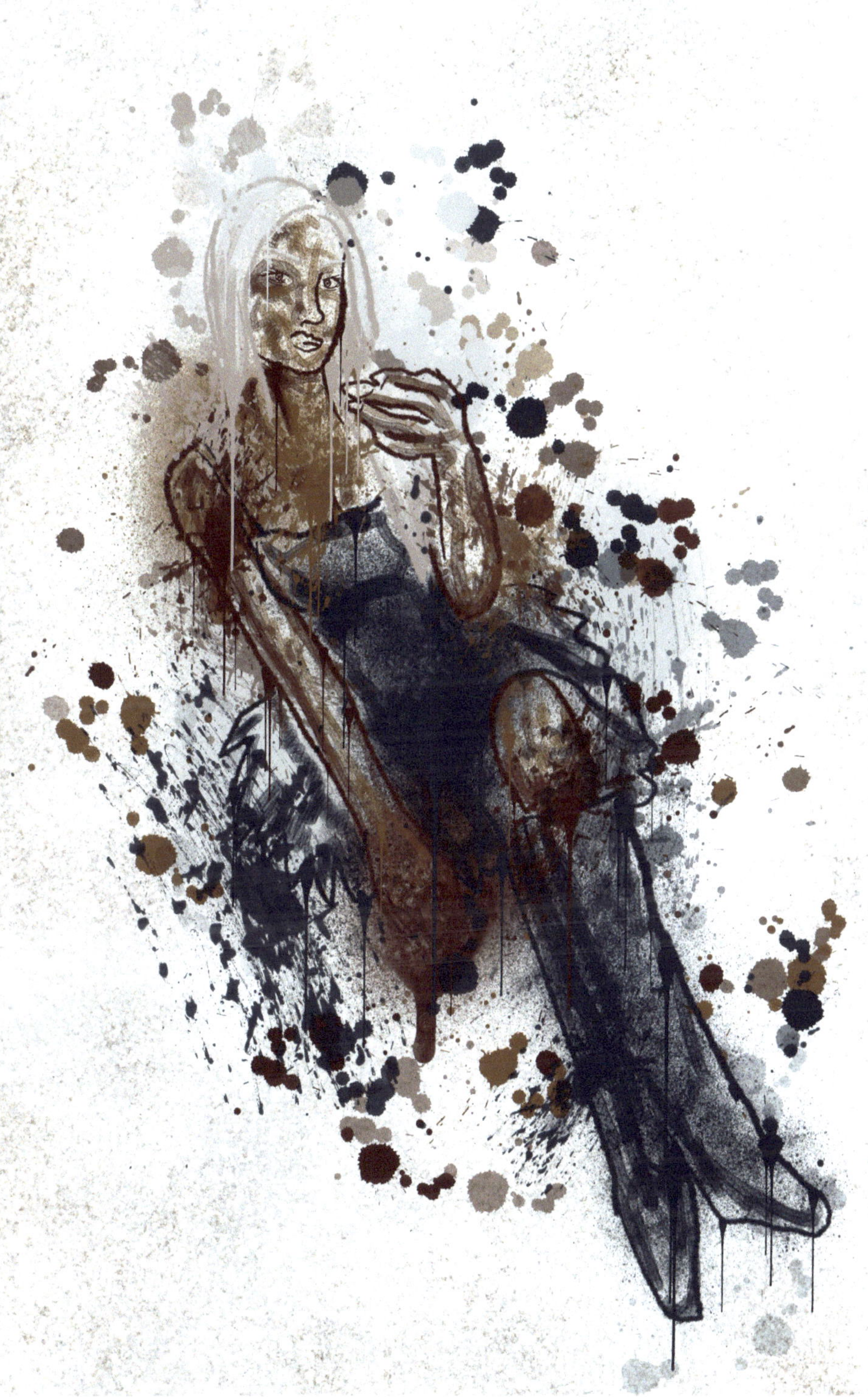

"C"
2020
Digital

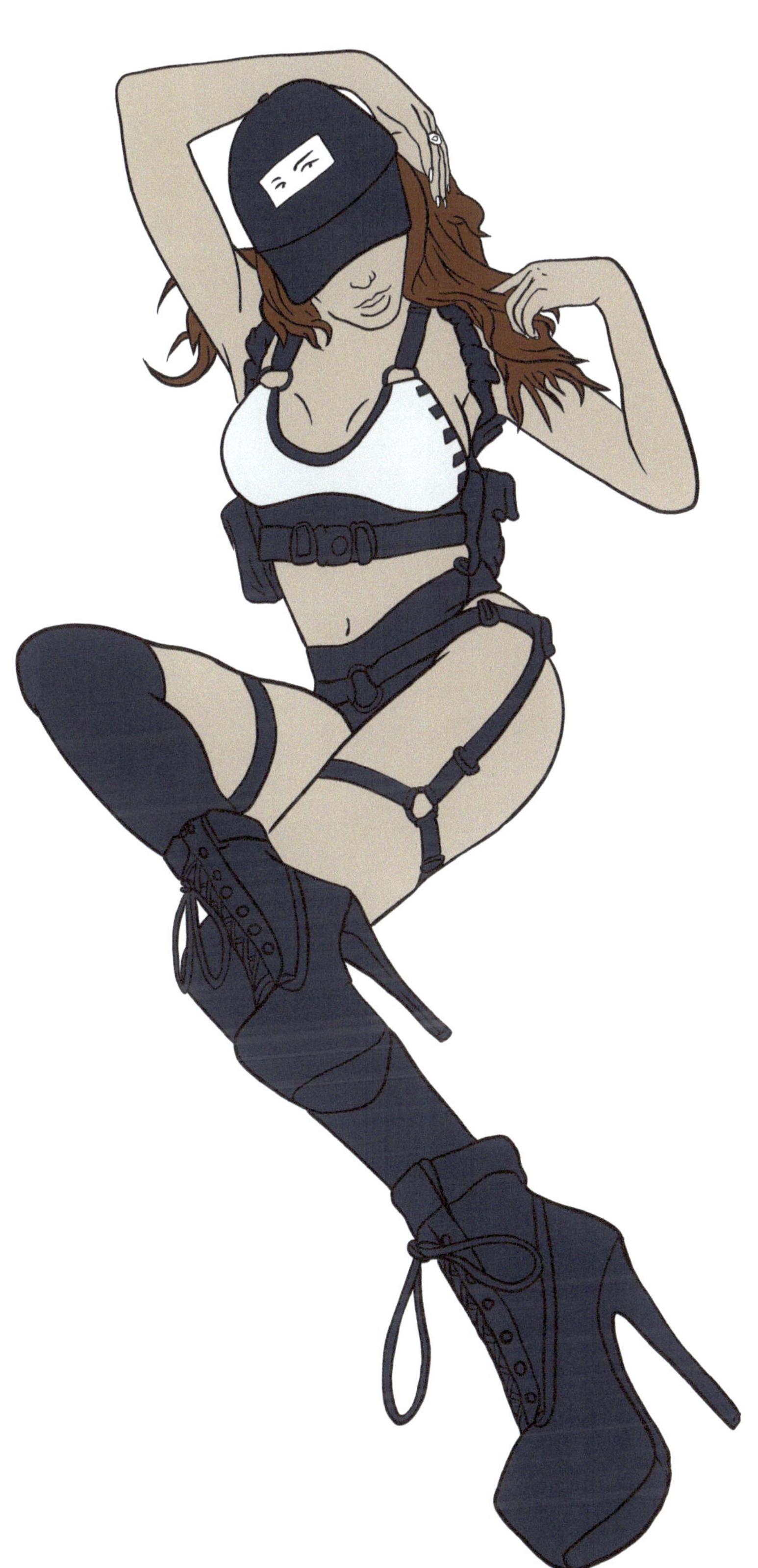

"Neon Rikku"
2019
Digital

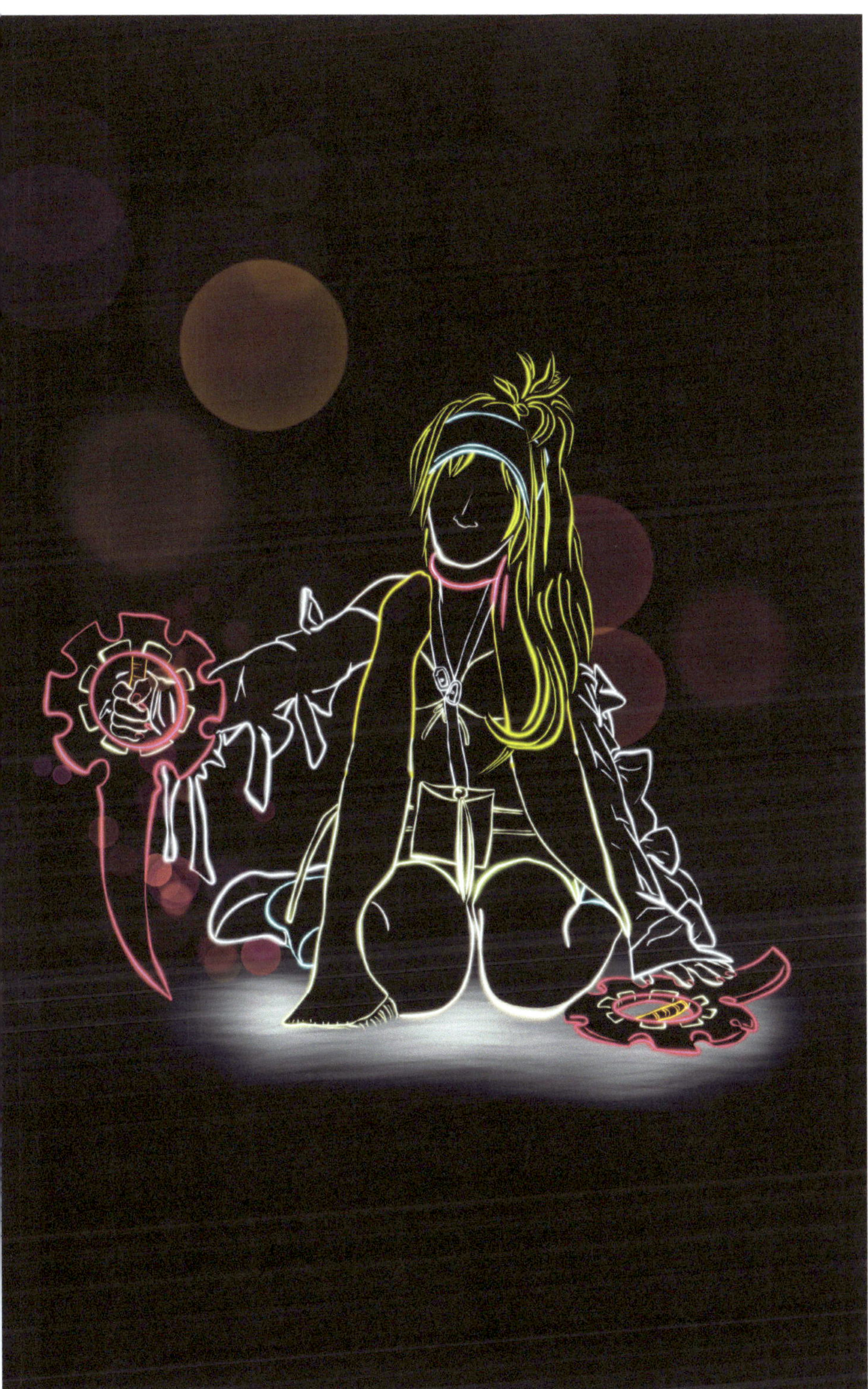

"Reflecting Pool Planet"
2019
Digital

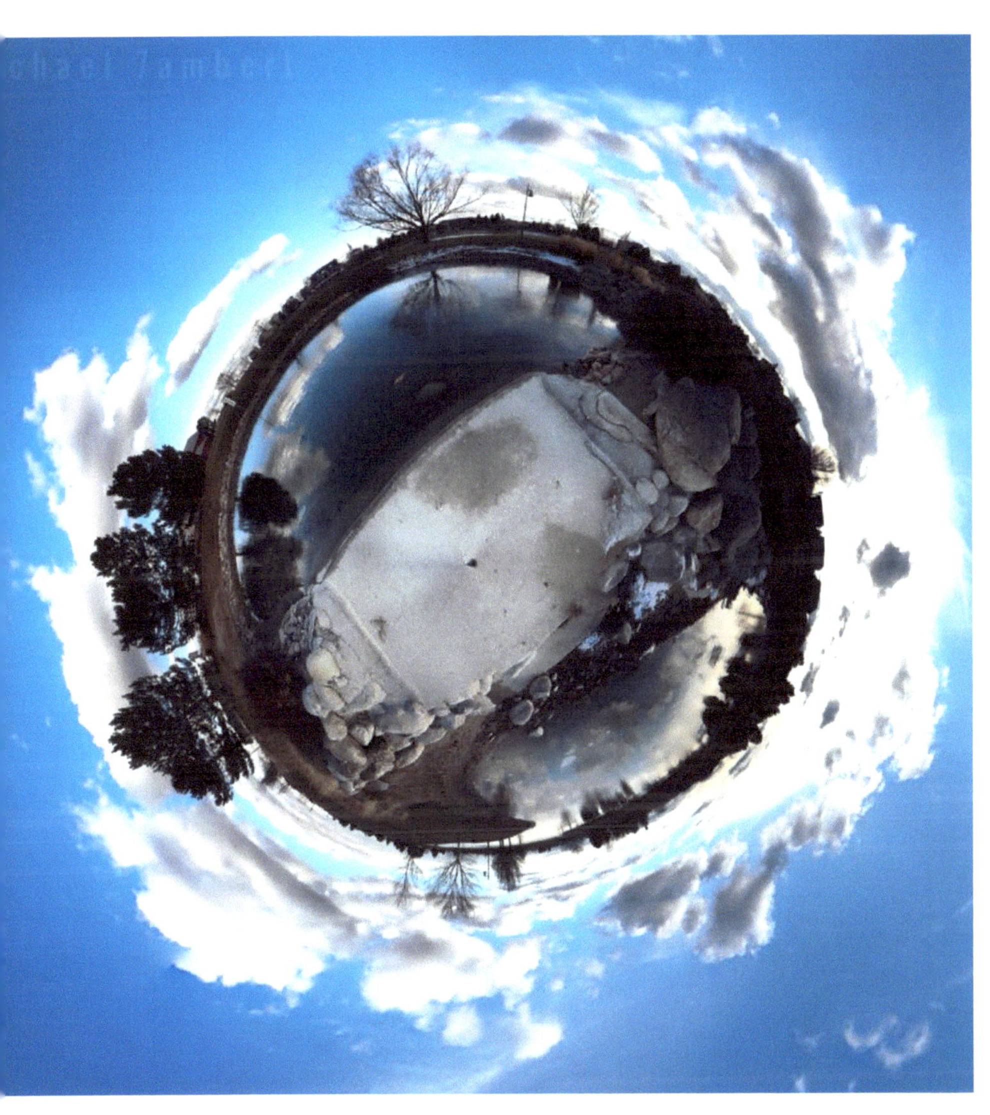

"Red Dress Girl"
2020
Digital

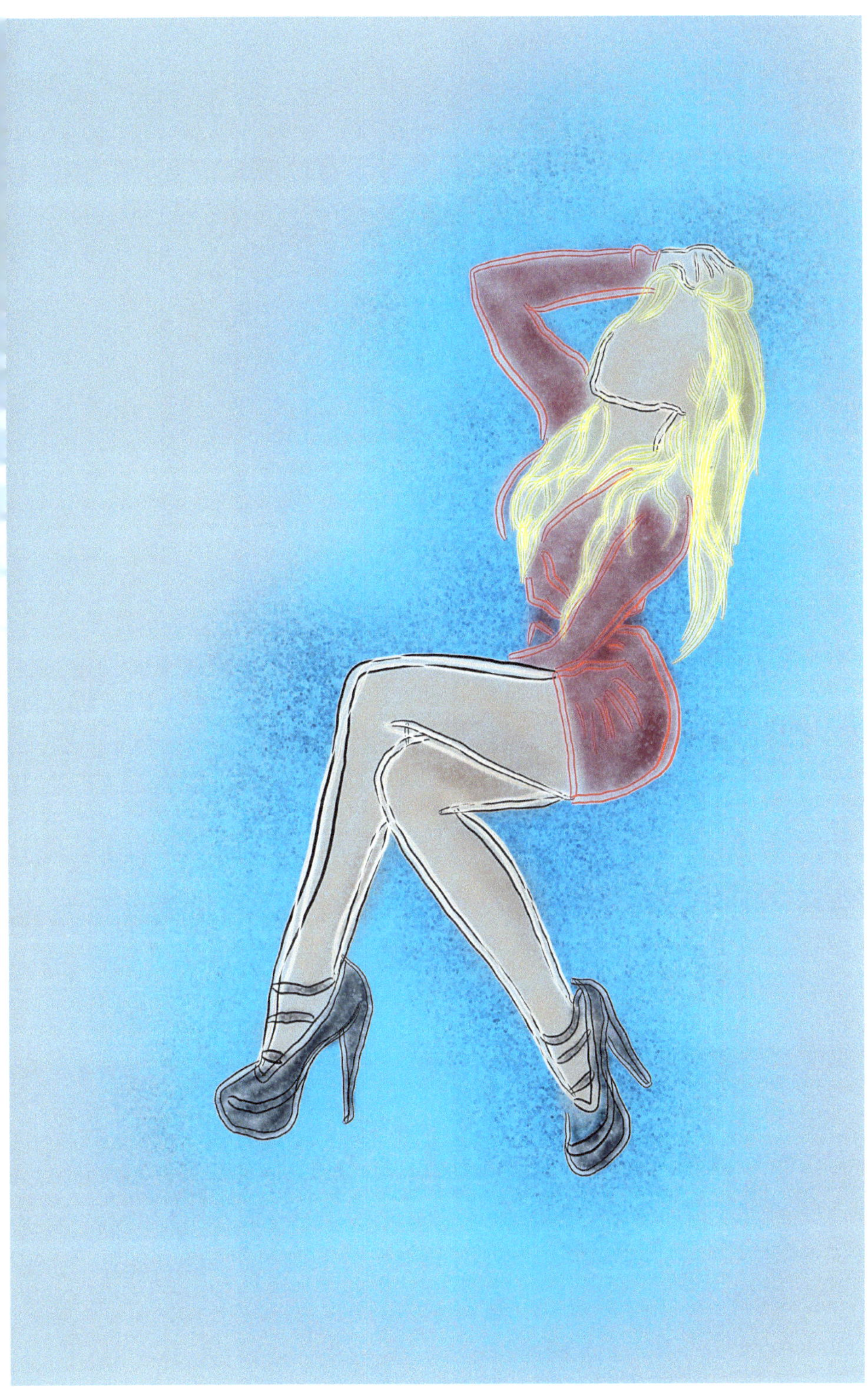

"Urban Girl #Orange"
2021
Digital

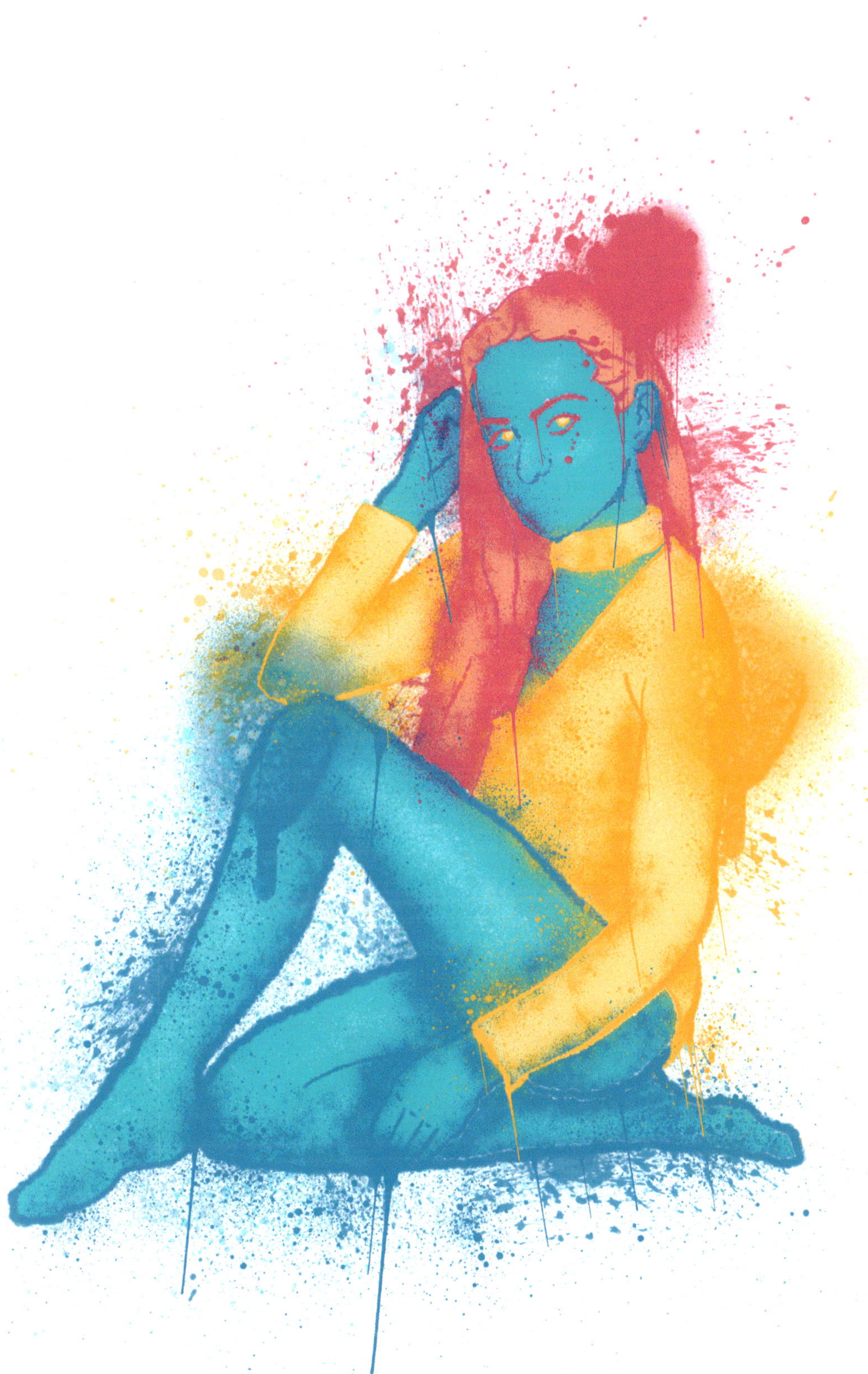

"Neon Yoga"
2020
Digital

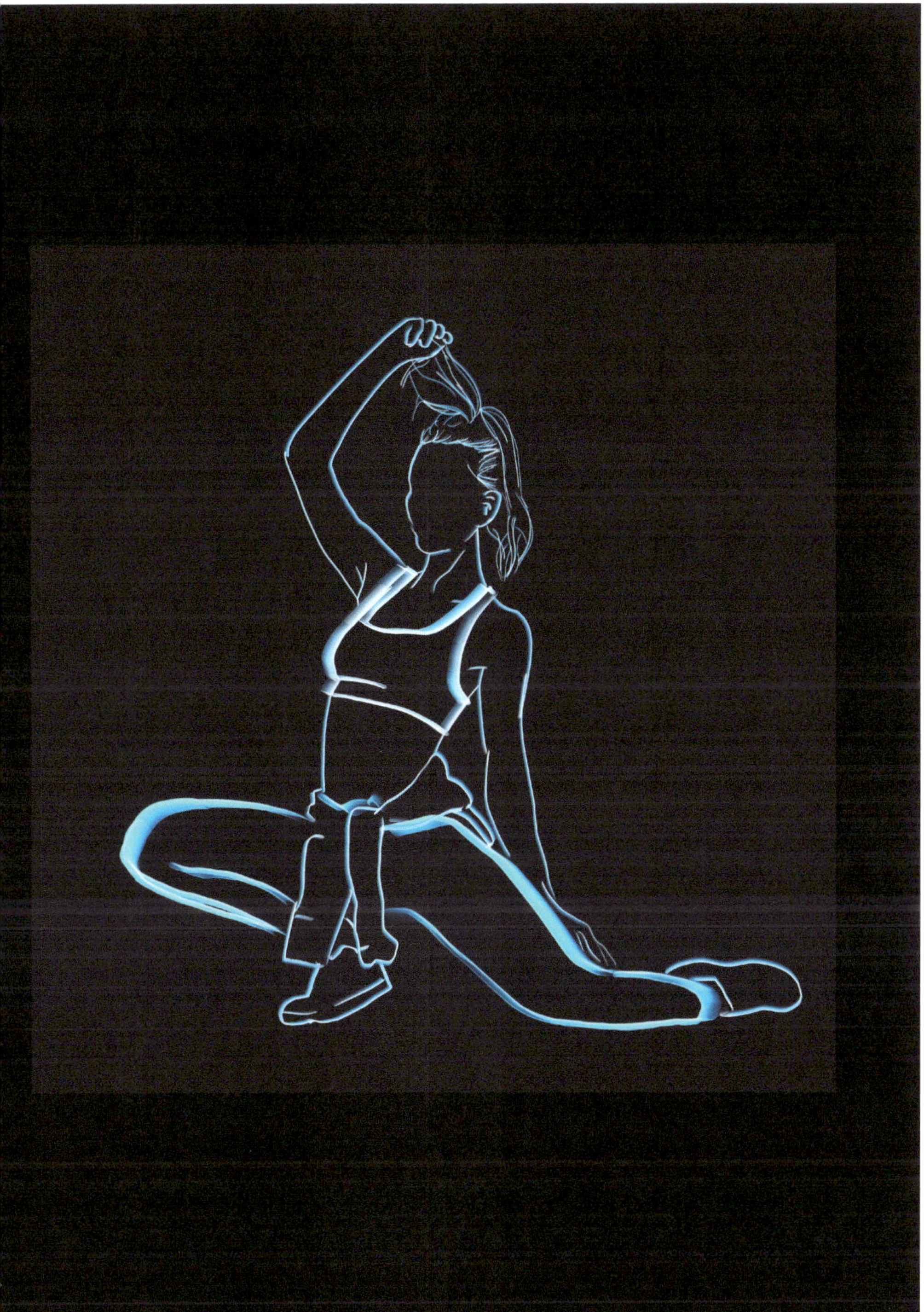

"Geometry Girl"
2020
Digital

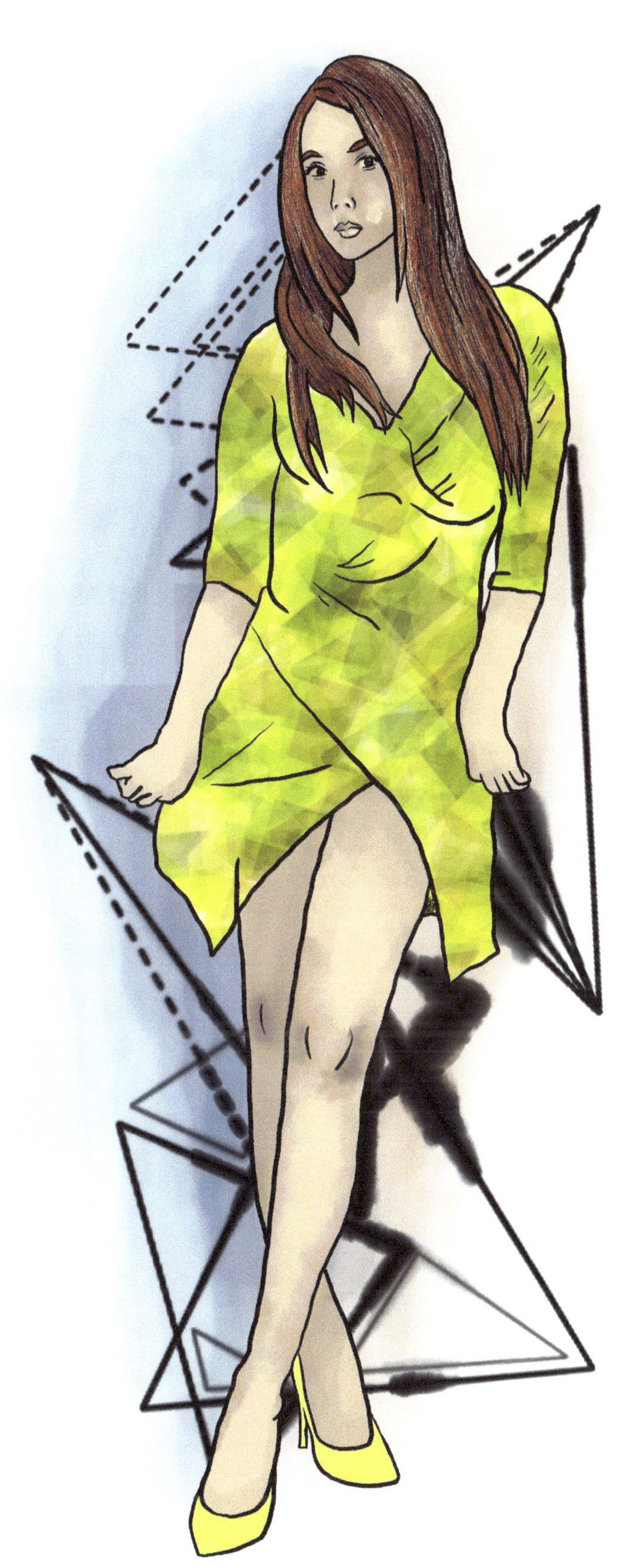

"Sports Girl"
2020
Digital

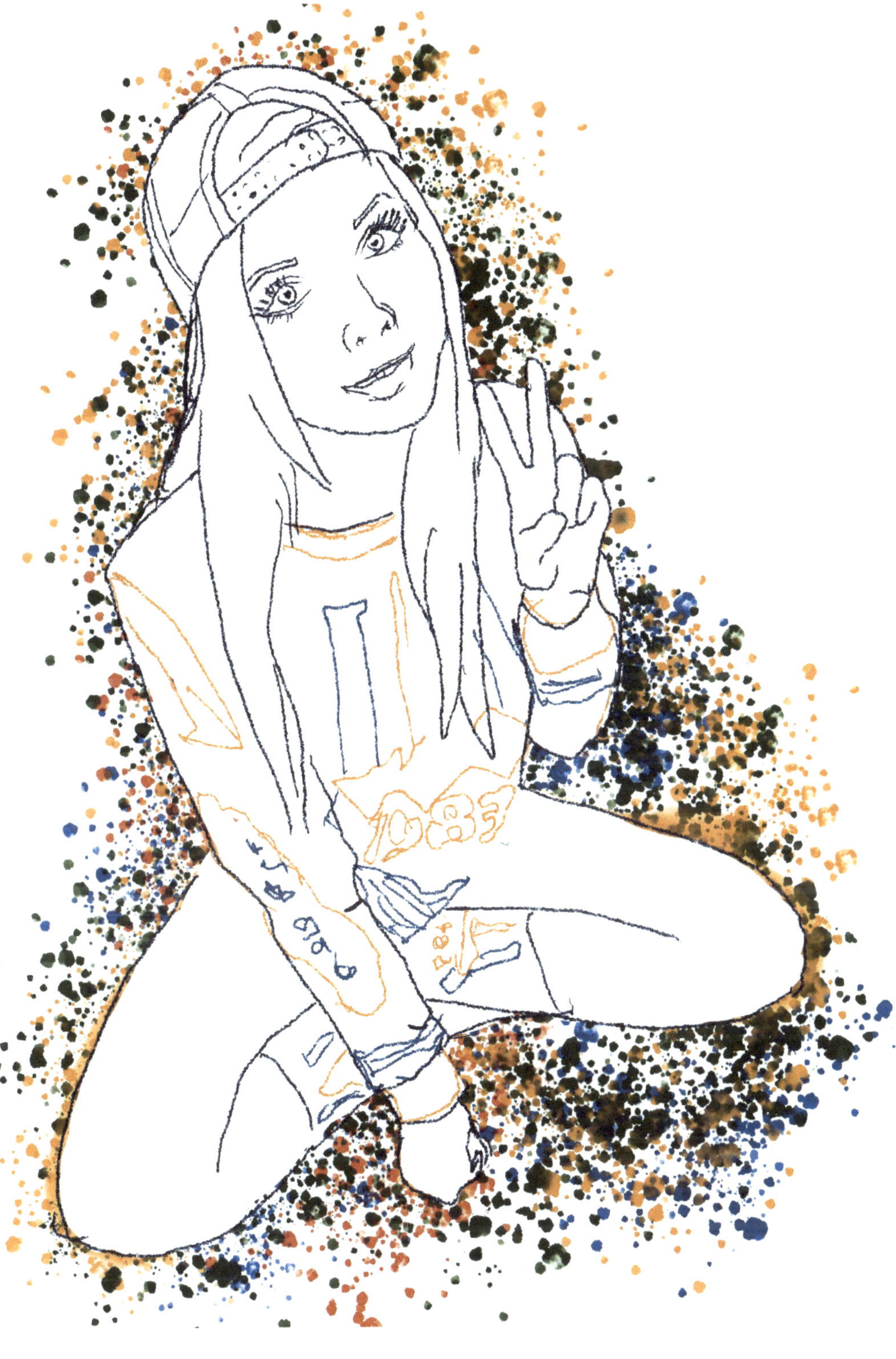

"Anatomy #Chest"
2021
Digital Illustration

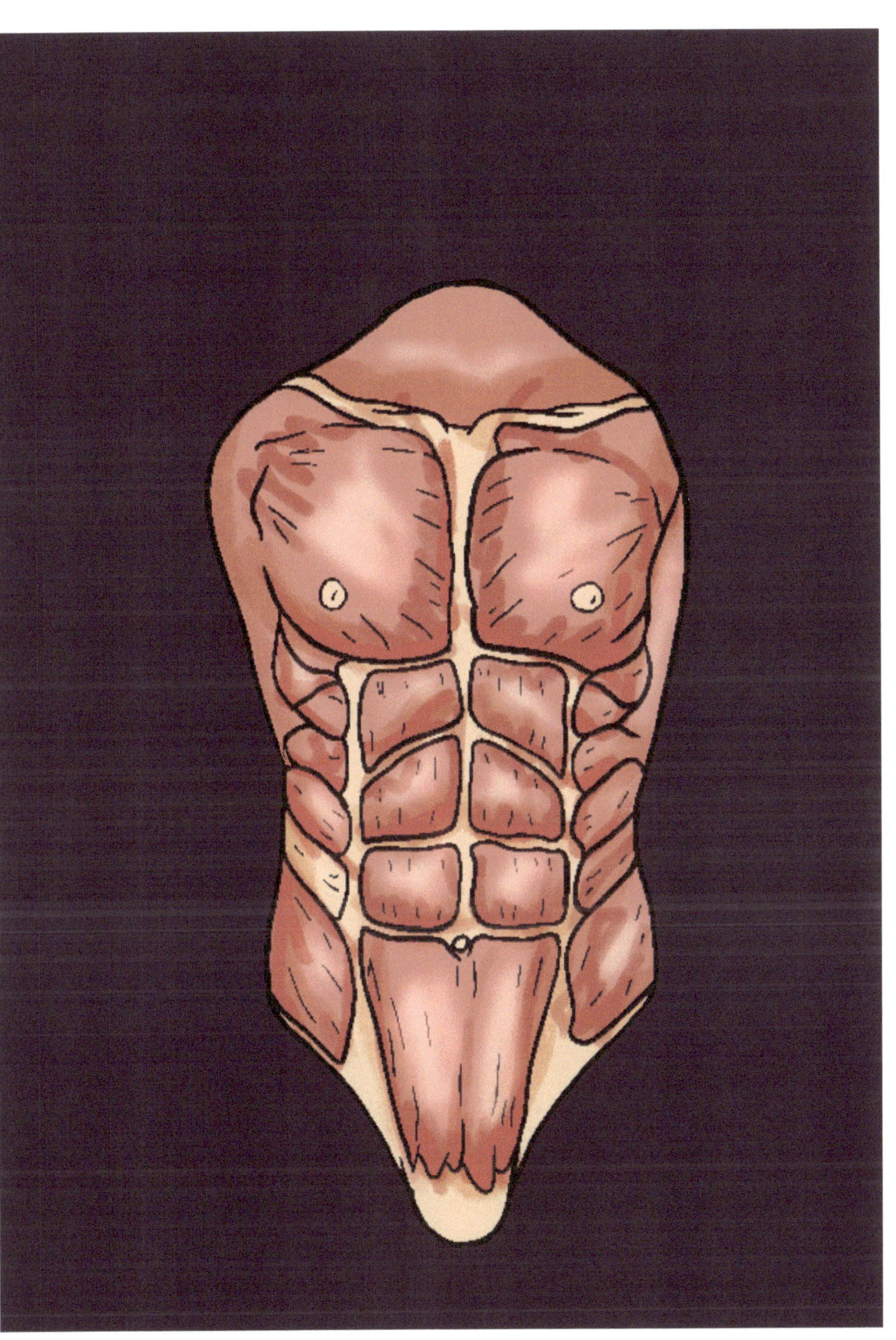

"Piano Music Visualizer #1"
2023
Digital, Photography, Animation and
Photo Manipulation

"Piano Music Visualizer #2"
2023
Digital, Photography, Animation and
Photo Manipulation

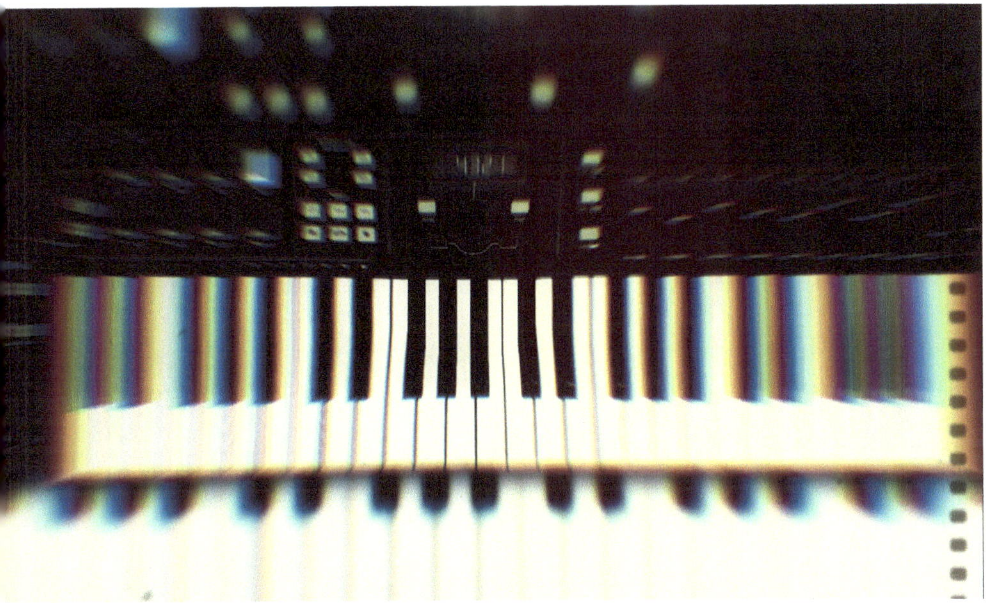

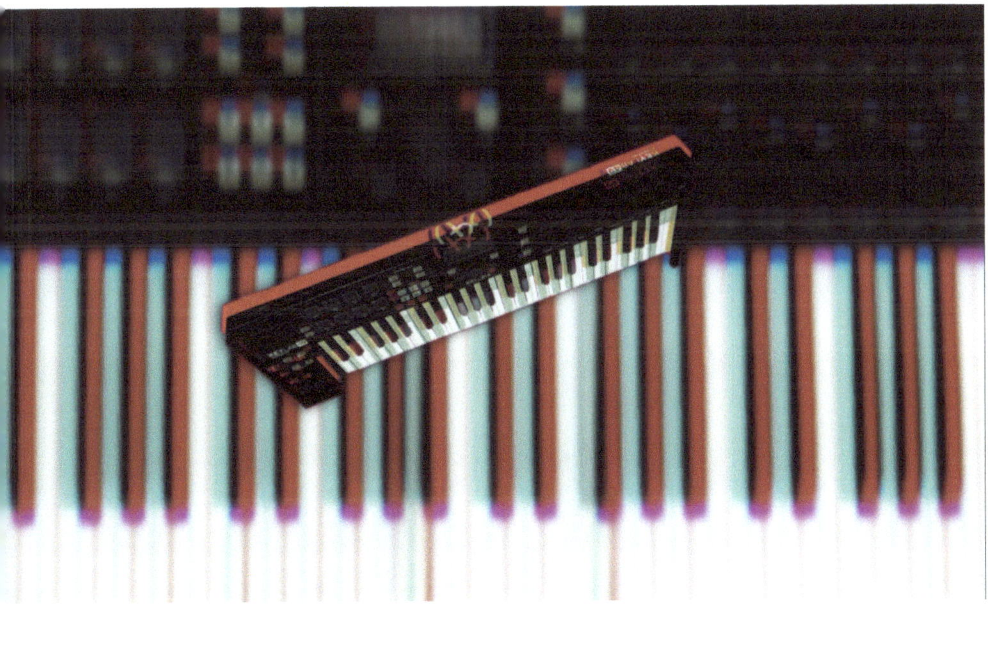

"Piano Music Visualizer #3"
2023
*Digital, Photography, Animation and
Photo Manipulation*

"Piano Music Visualizer #4"
2023
*Digital, Photography, Animation and
Photo Manipulation*

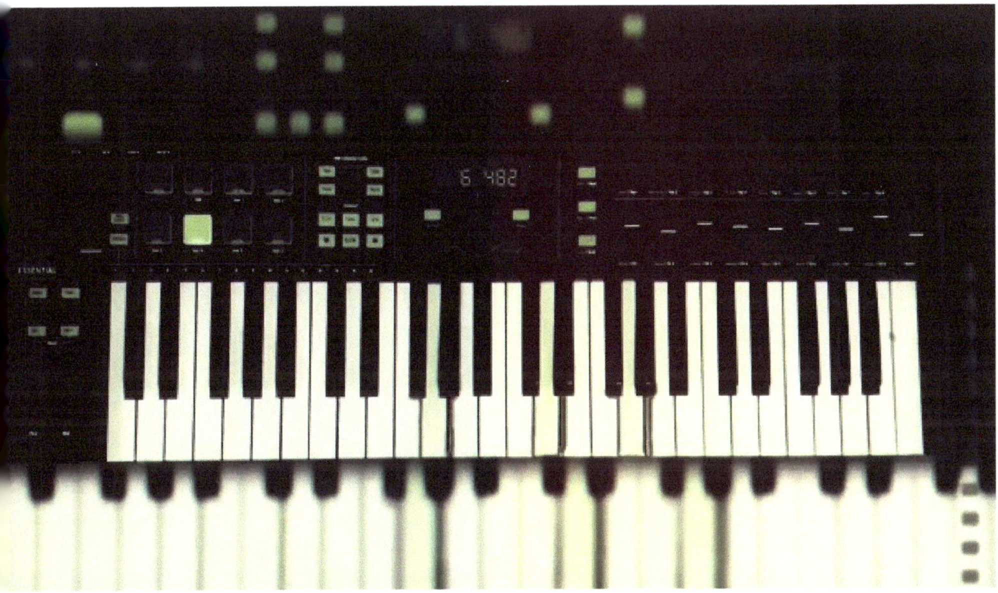

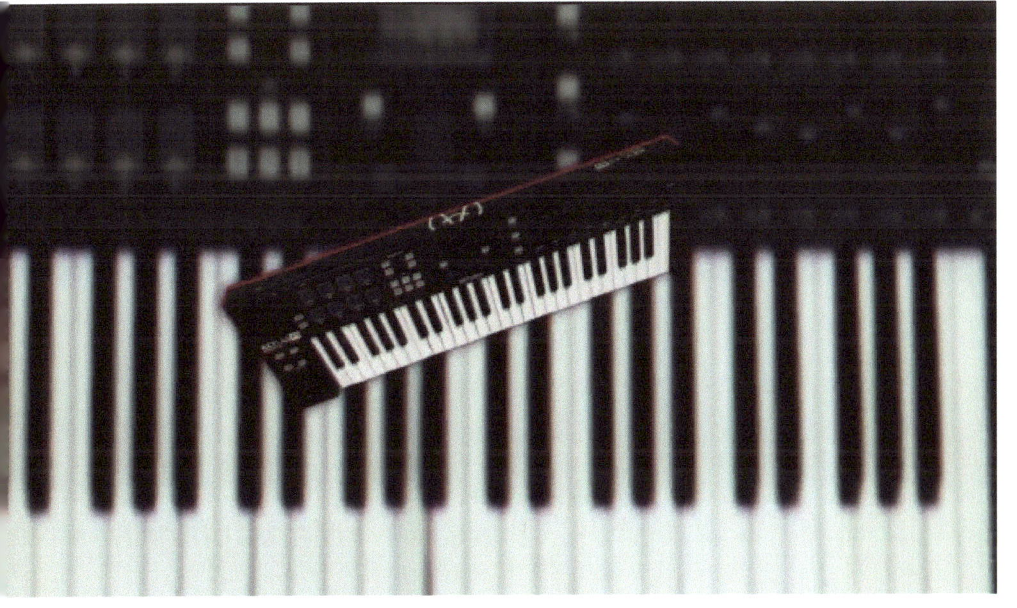

"Piano Music Visualizer #5"
2023
Digital, Animation and Photo
Manipulation

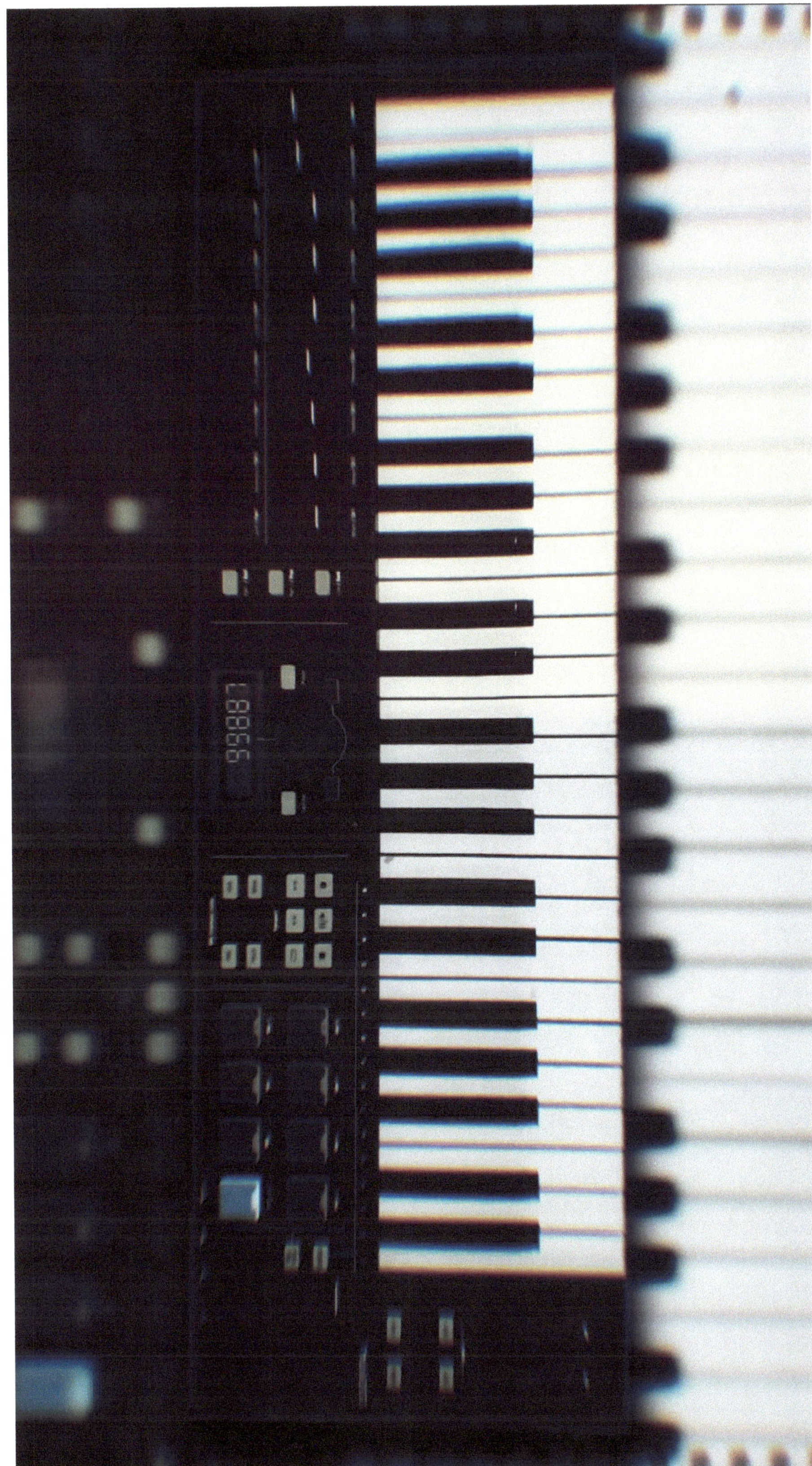

"Custom Guitar #1"
2022
Photography

"Custom Guitar #2"
2022
Photography

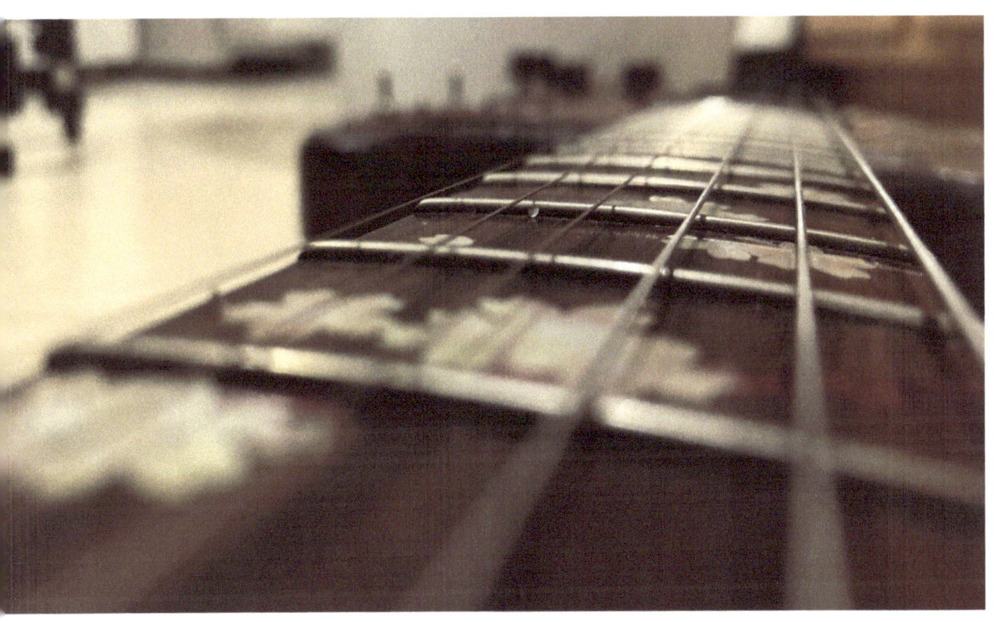

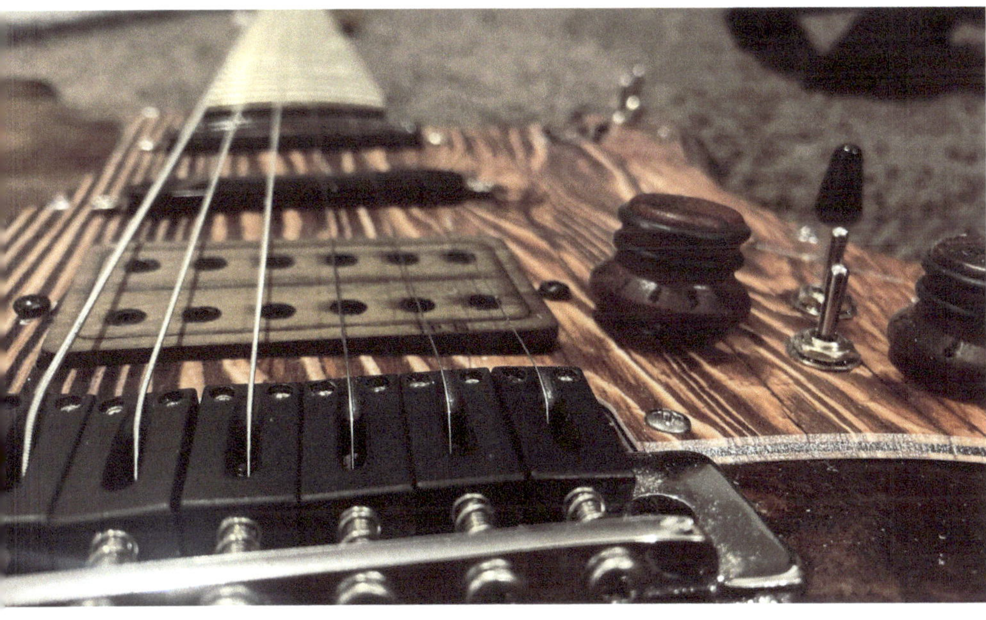

"Avalanca & Snowlight #1"
2018
Game

"Avalanca & Snowlight #2"
2018
Game

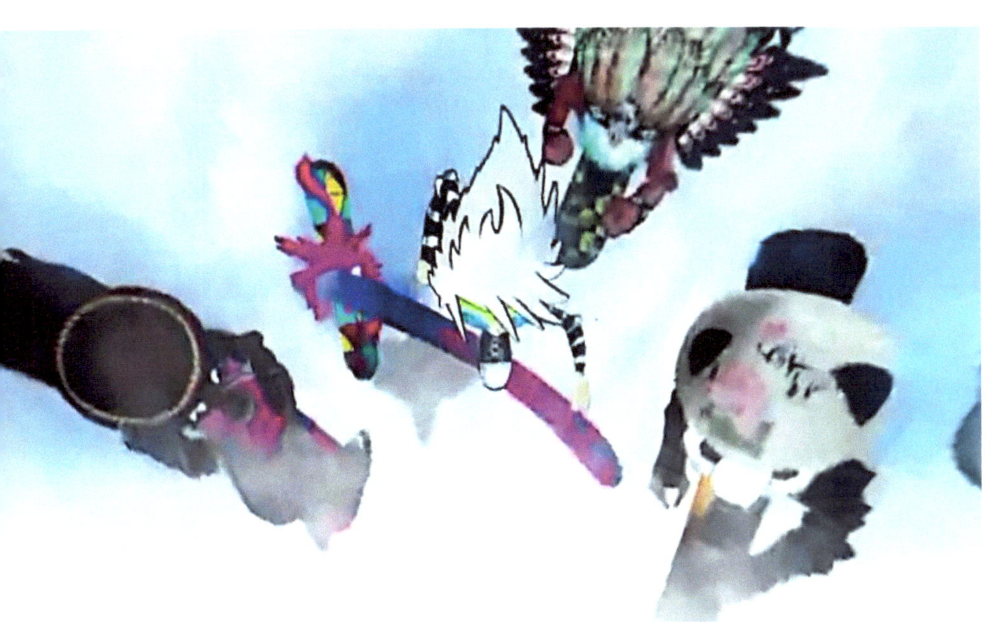

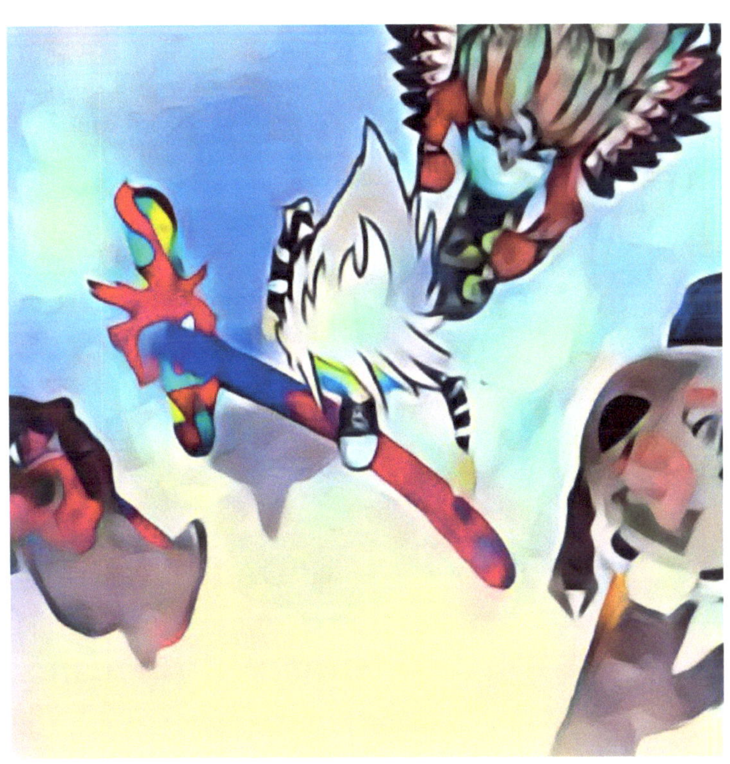

DeathWish #1”
2018
Illustration & Animation

“DeathWish #2”
2018
Illustration & Animation

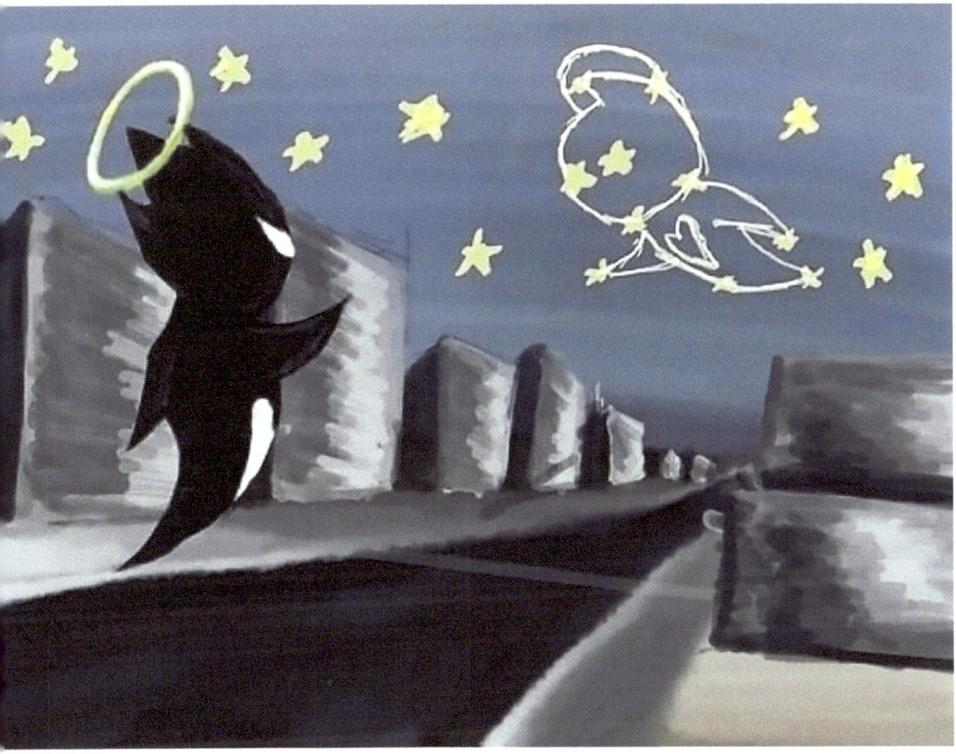

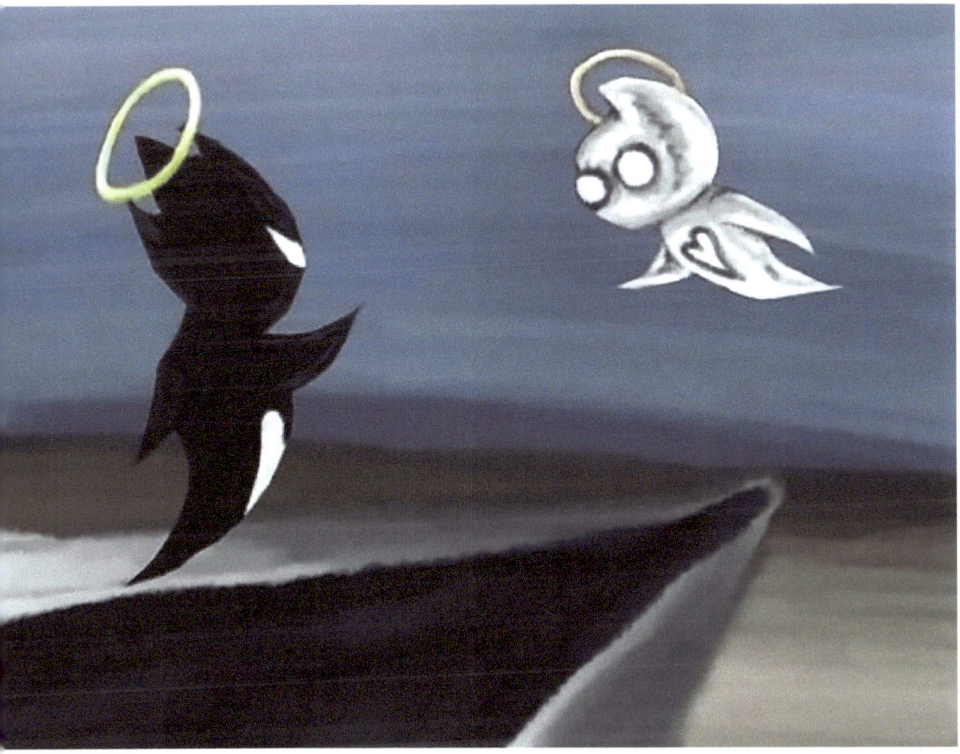

"DeathWish Promo"
2019
Digital

"Pear"
2020
Digital Illustration

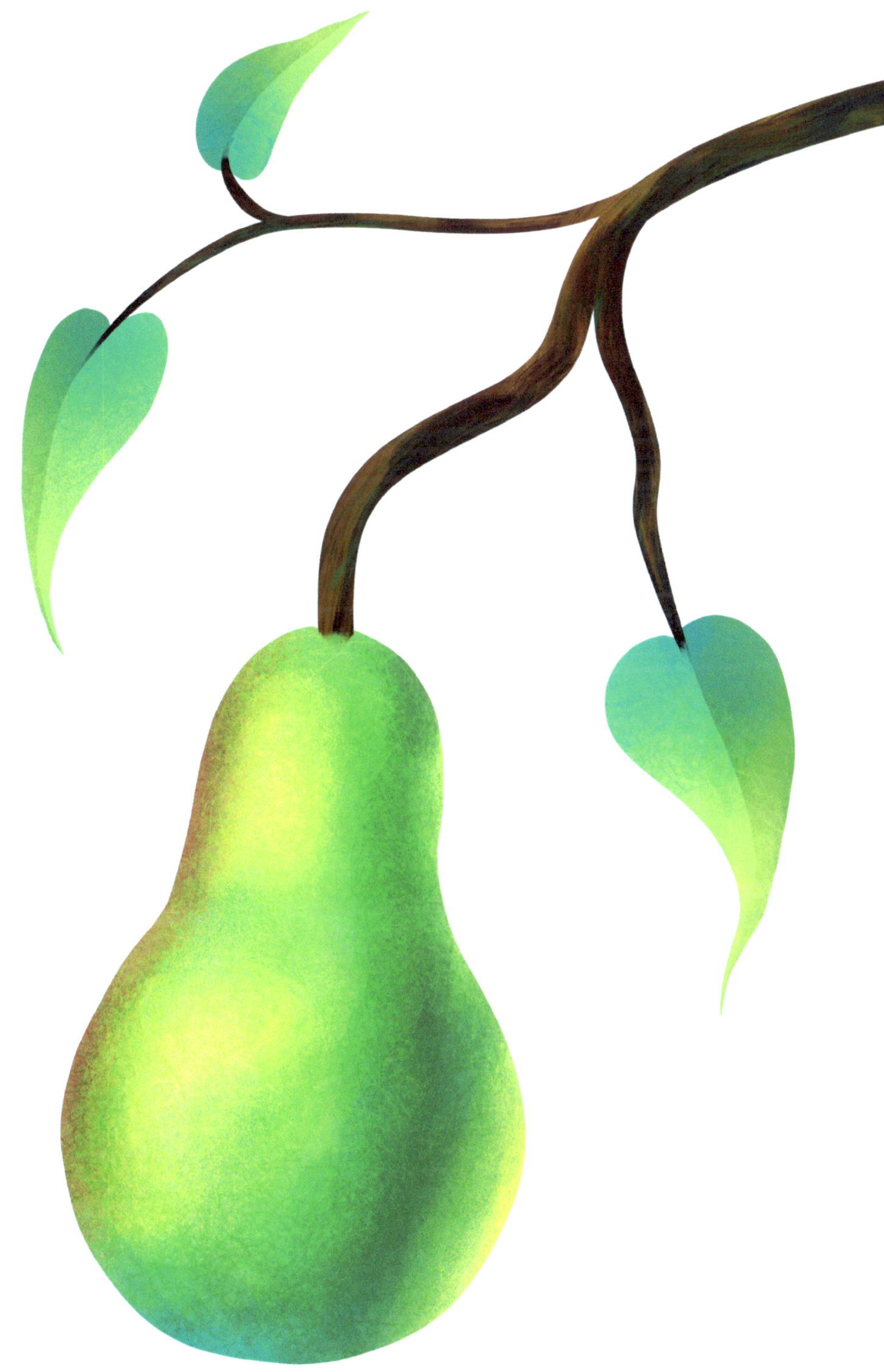

"Ponder"
2021
Digital Illustration

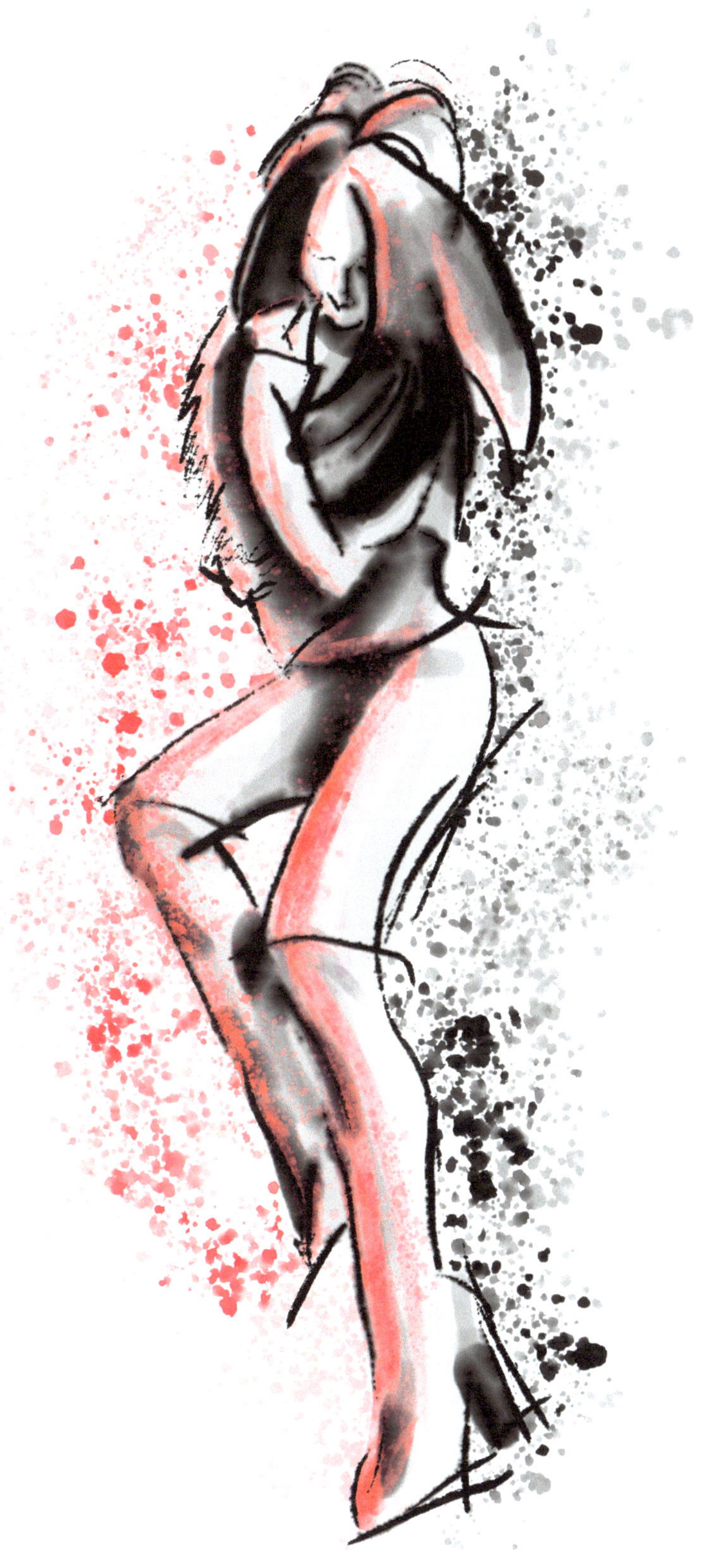

"Piranha"
2016
Digital Illustration

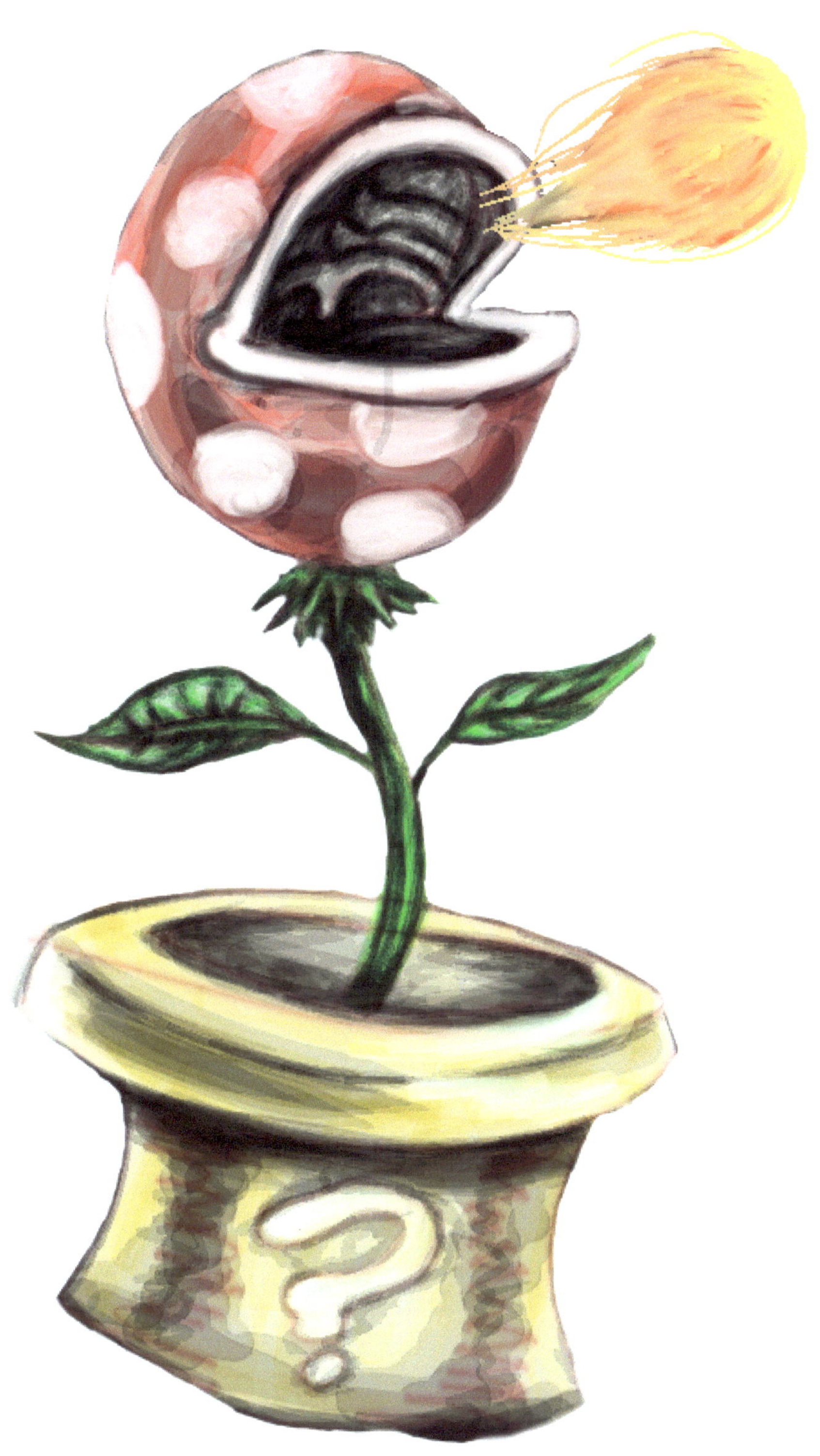

"Urban Girl #LightGreen"
2020
Digital Illustration

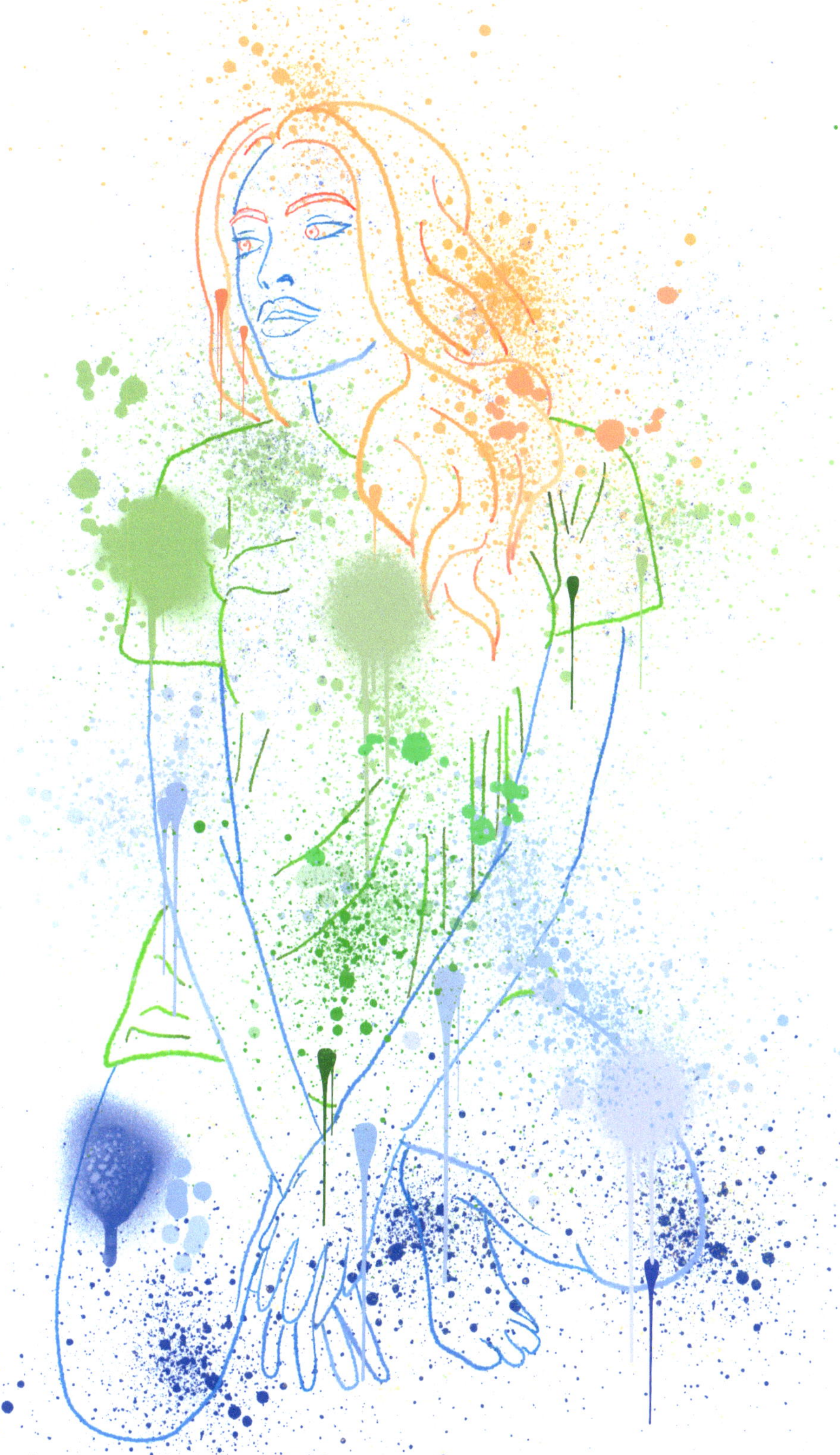

"The Arctic Saturn"
2018
Digital Illustration

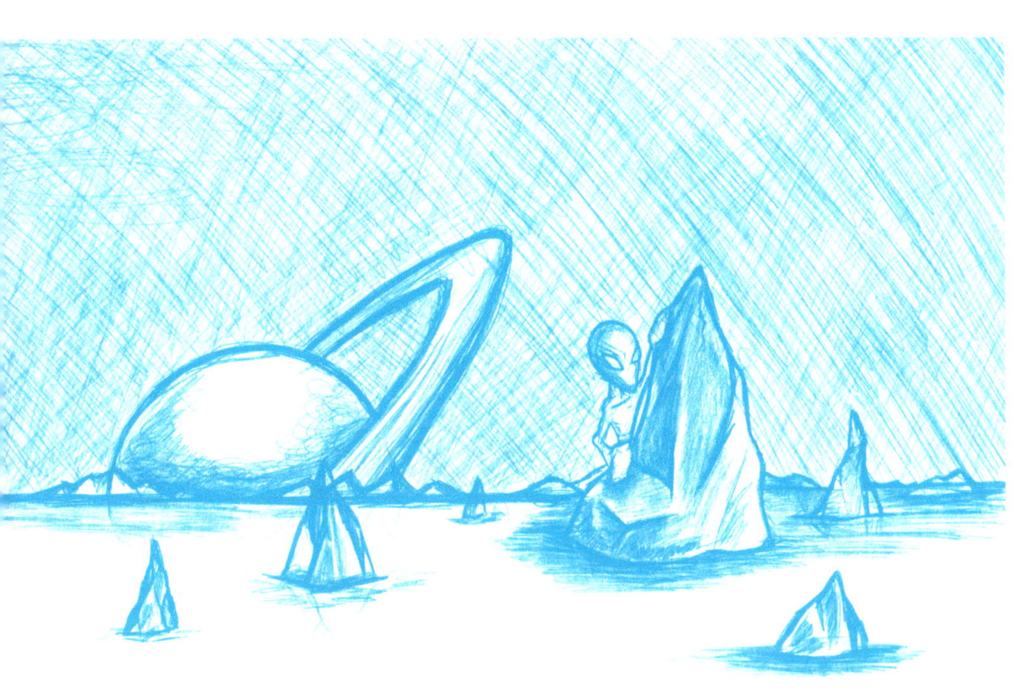

"Ninjas of Alaska"
2020
Digital Illustration

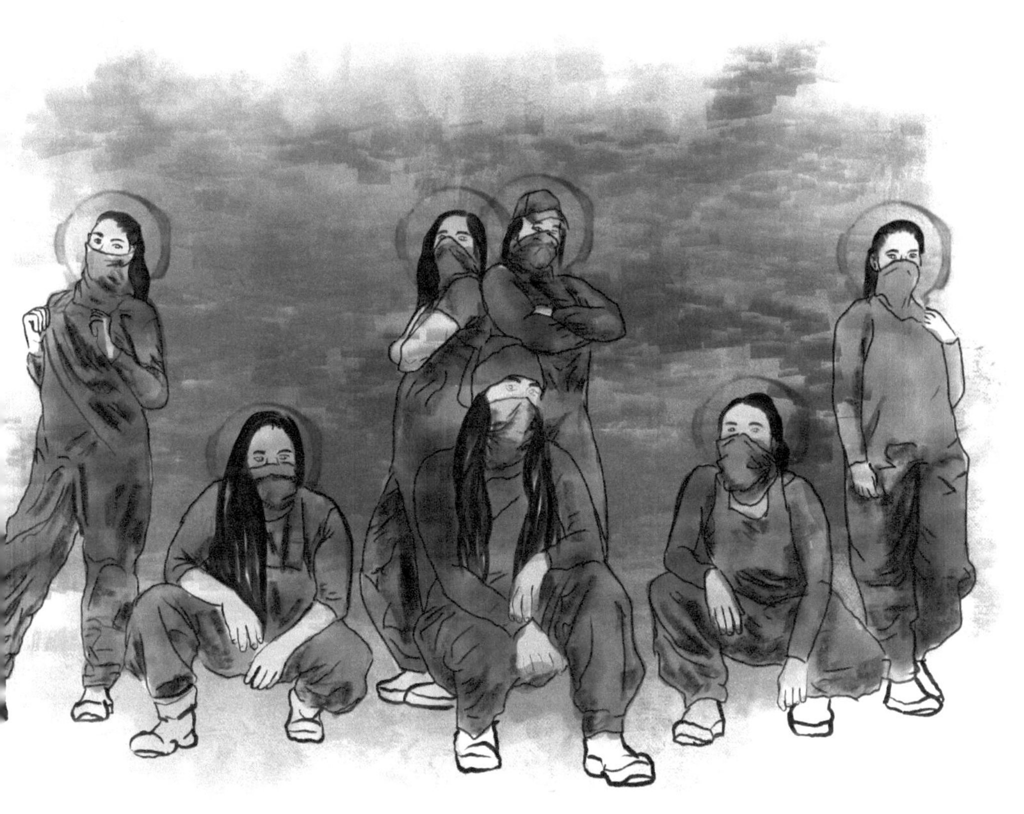

"Guitar"
2020
Digital Illustration

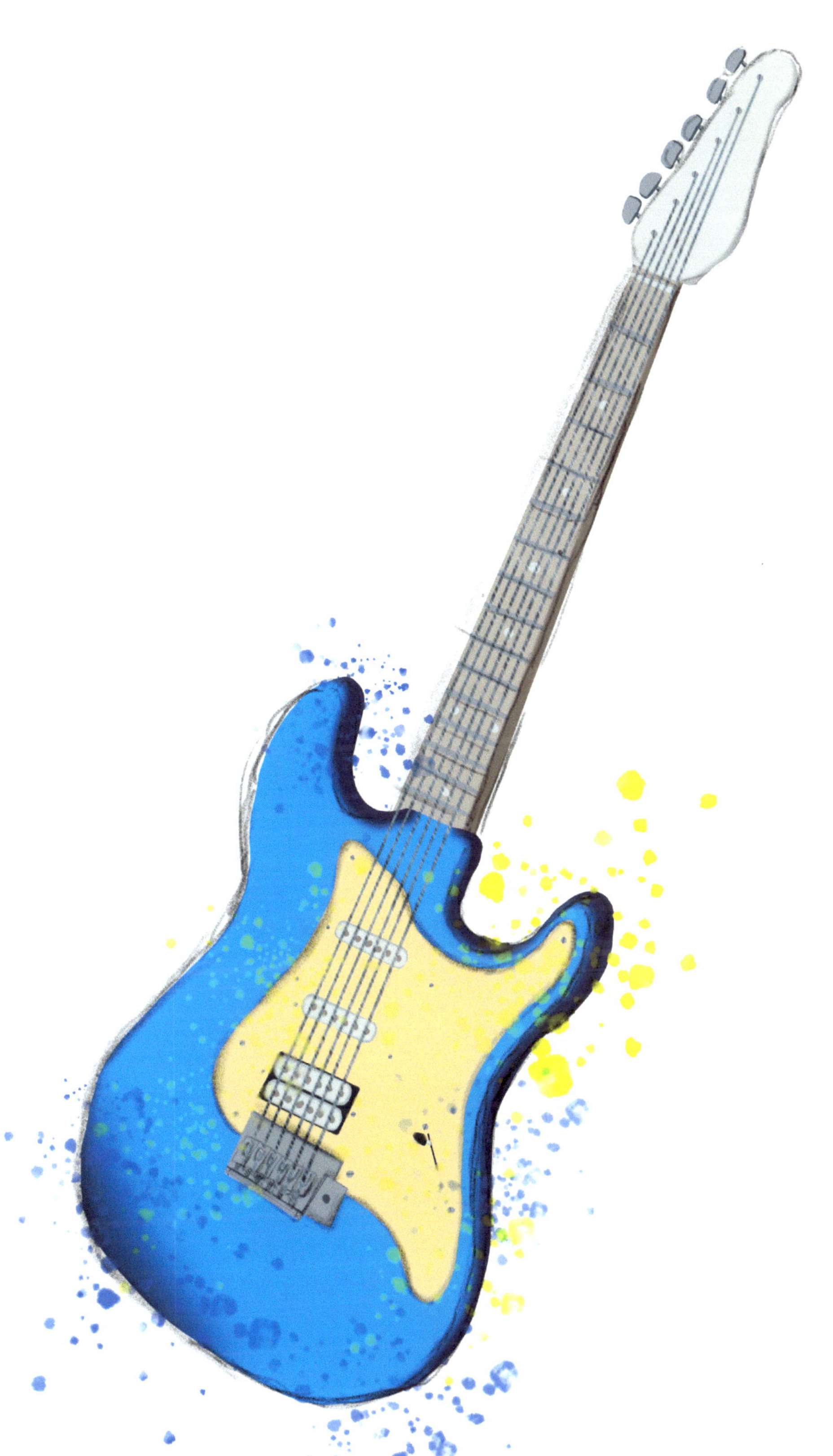

"Vacation"
2021
Digital Illustration

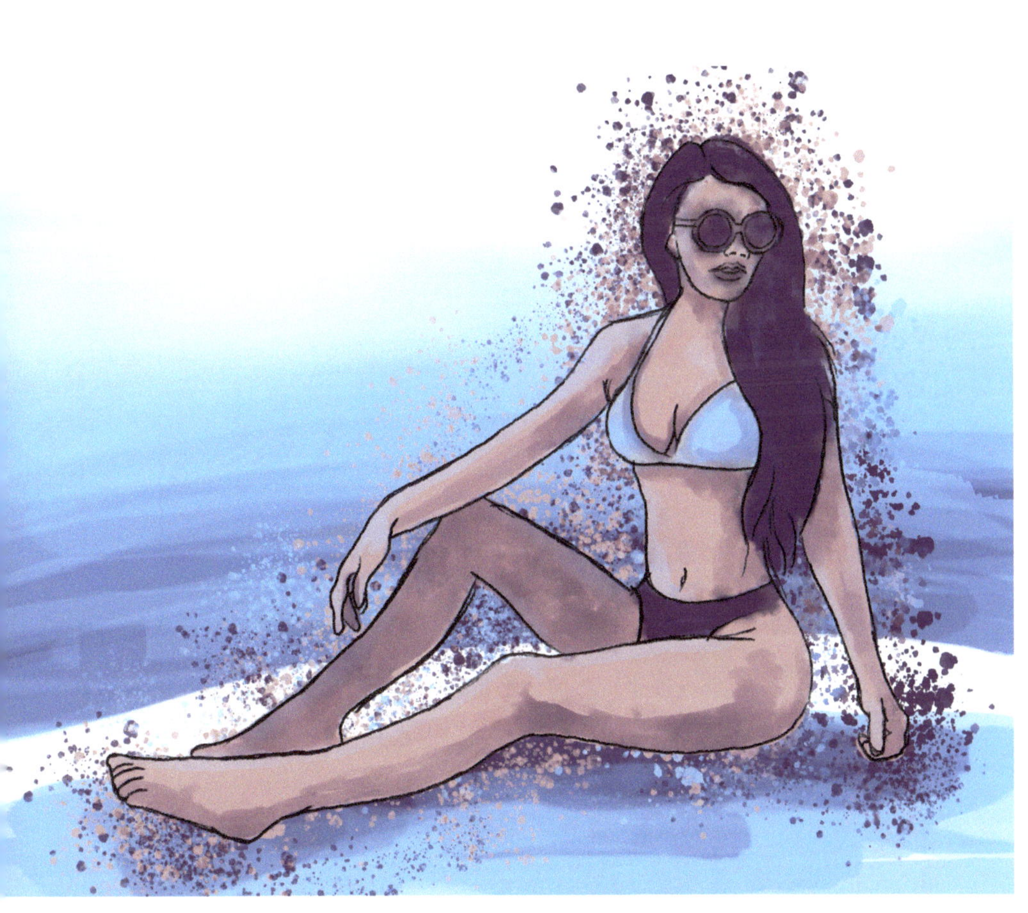

"Winter's Solance"
2022
Digital Illustration

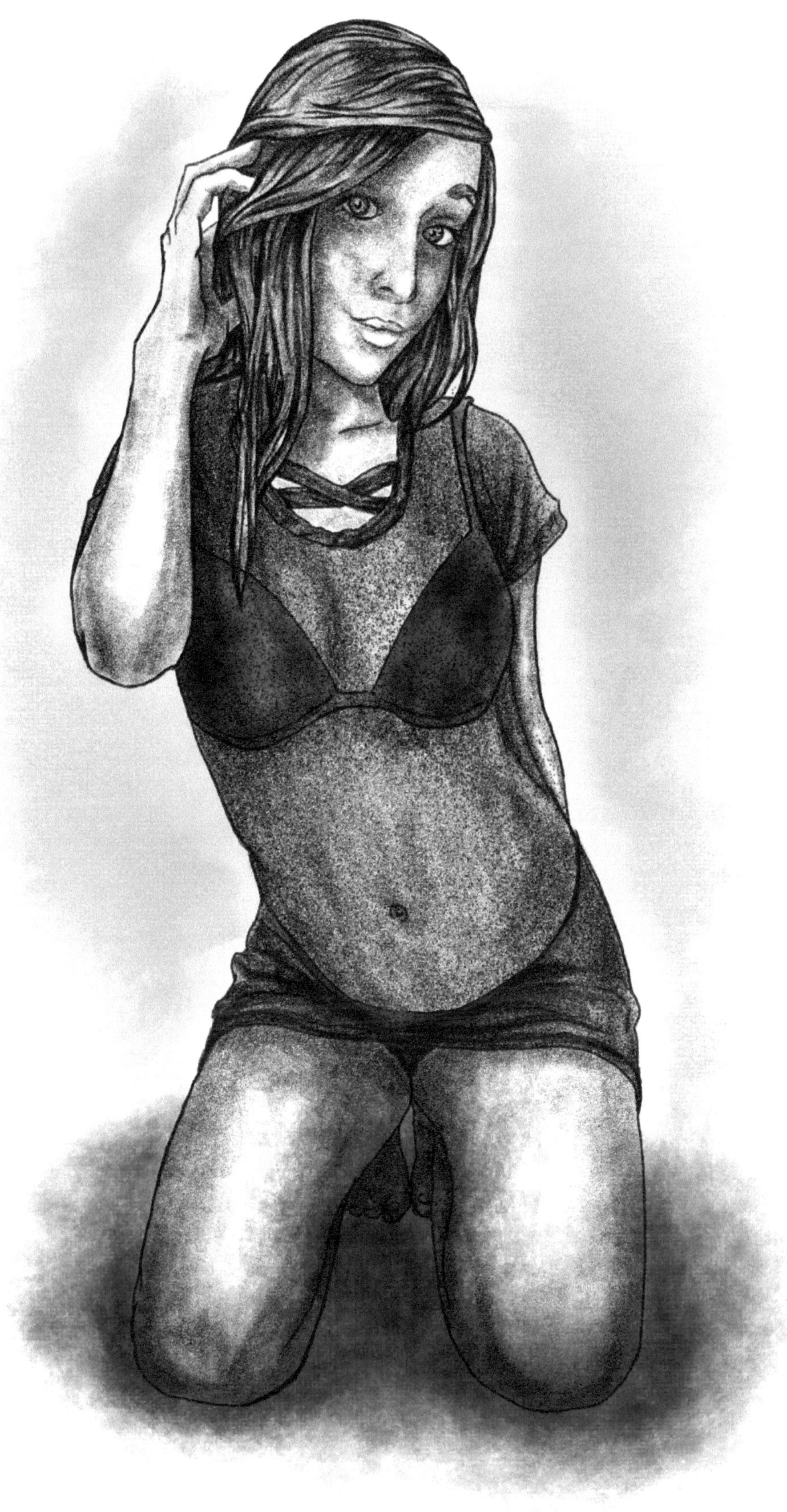

"Cherry Tree"
2020
Digital Illustration

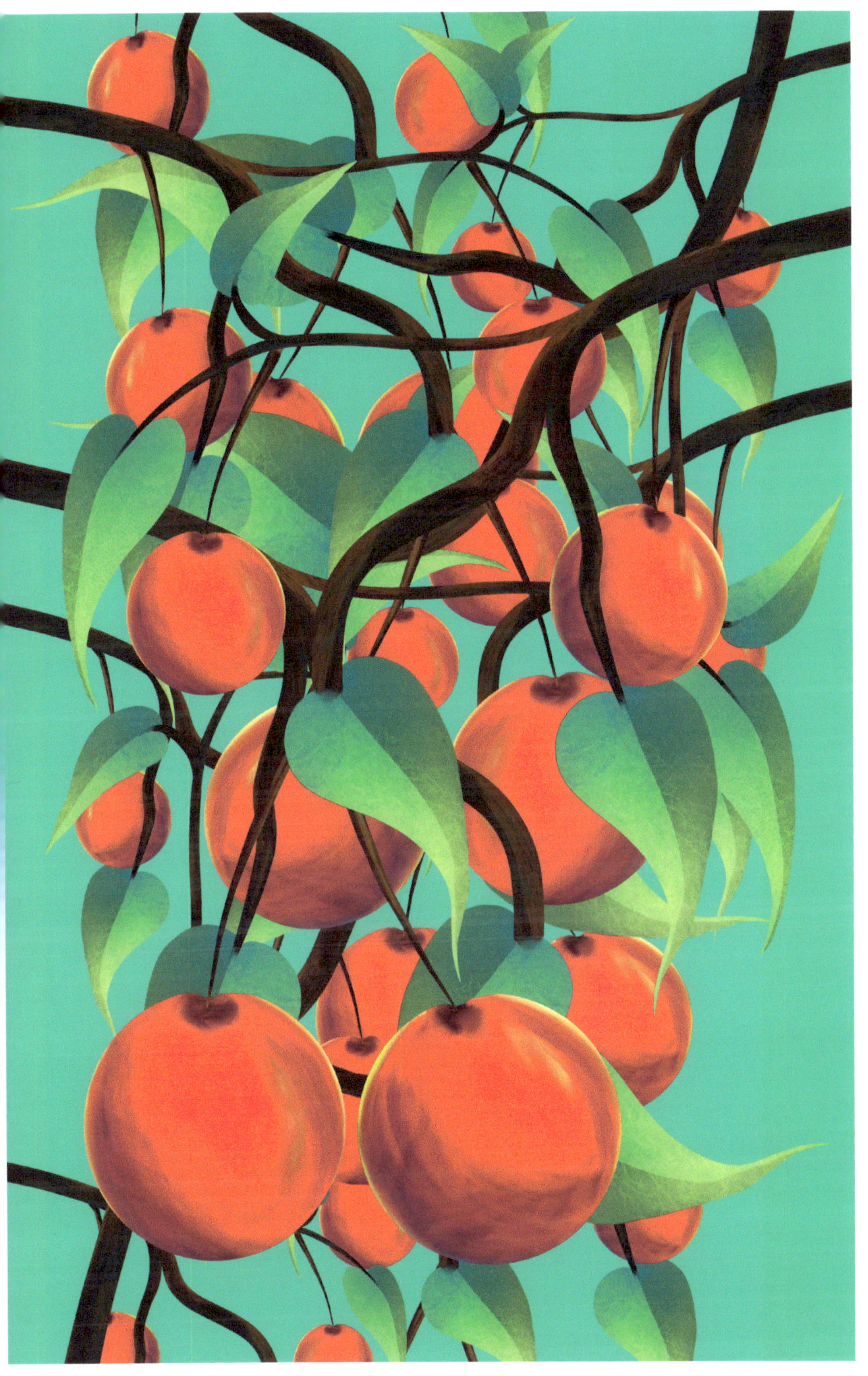

"Abstract Spraycan"
2024
Sharpie

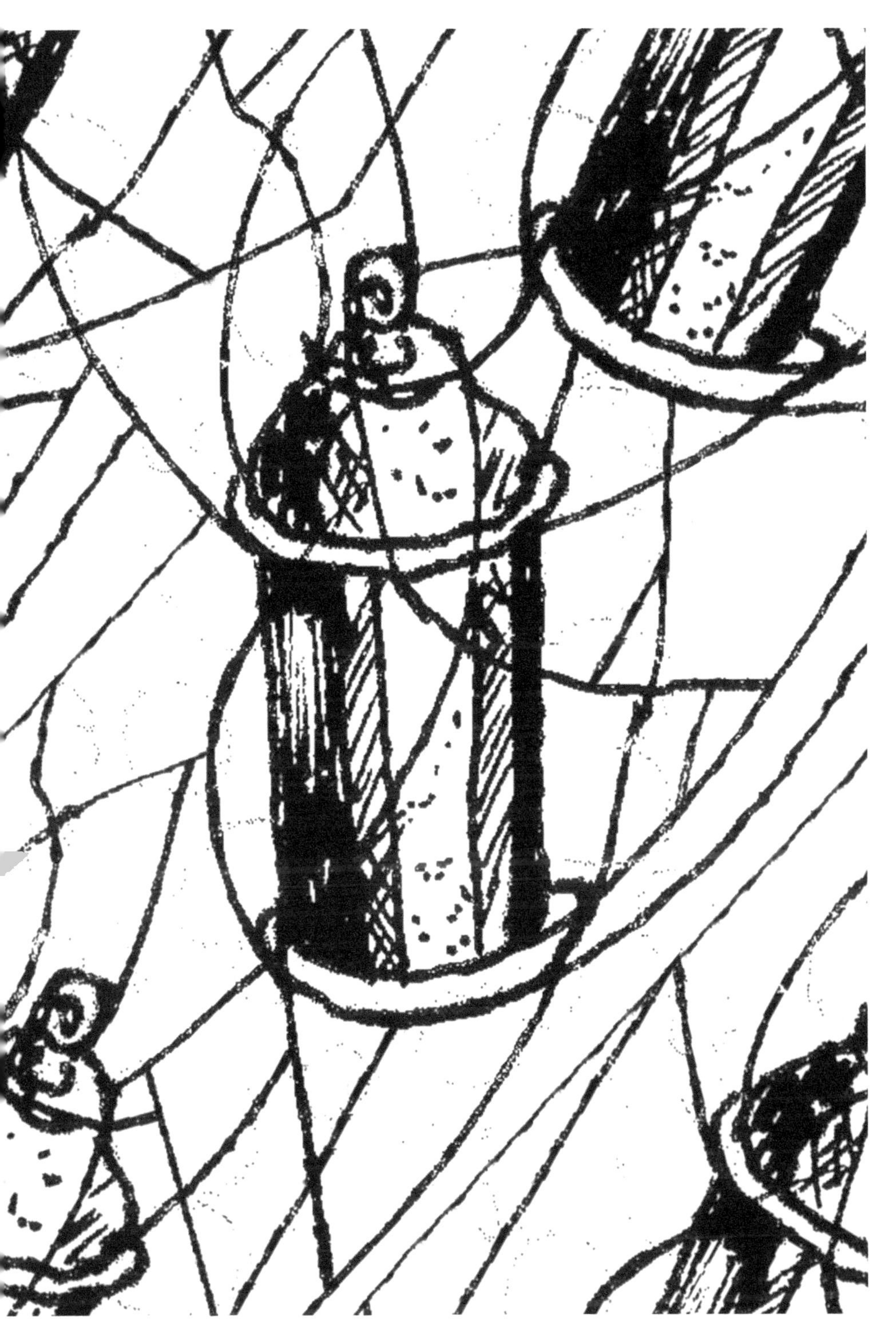

"Pear Tree"
2022
Digital Illustration

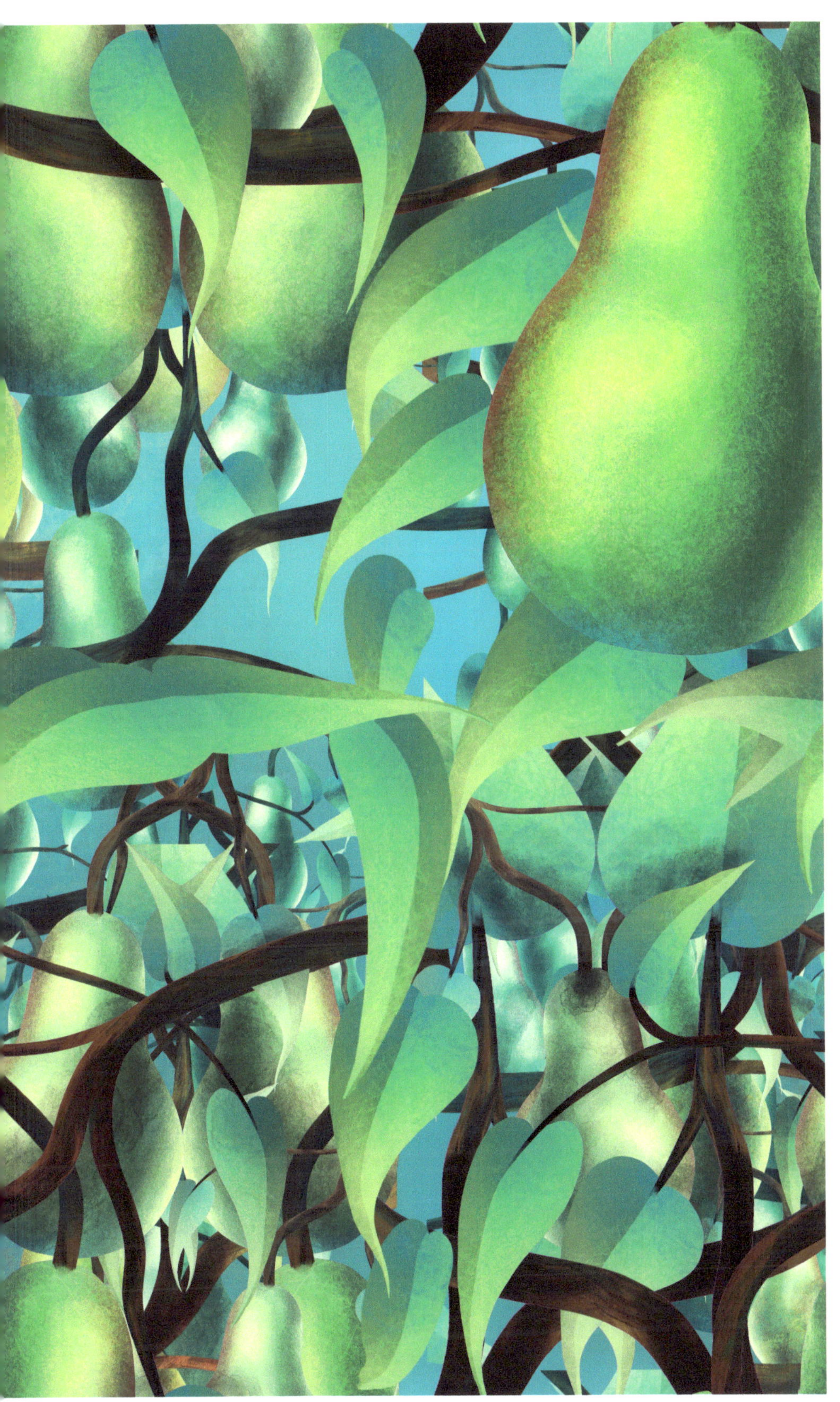

"Astro Auro"
2022
Acrylic

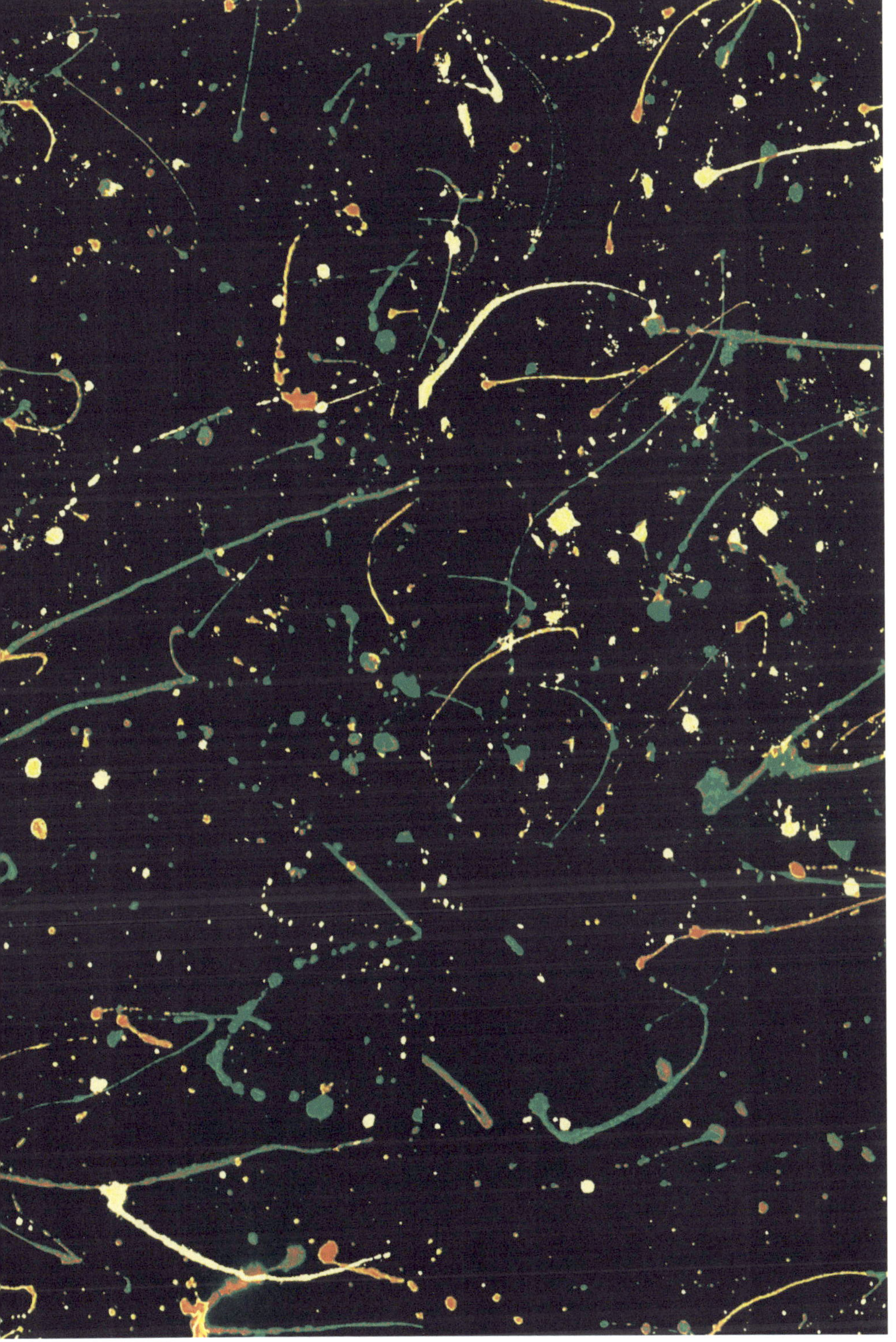

"Red Abstract Spray Paint Can"
2023
Sharpie

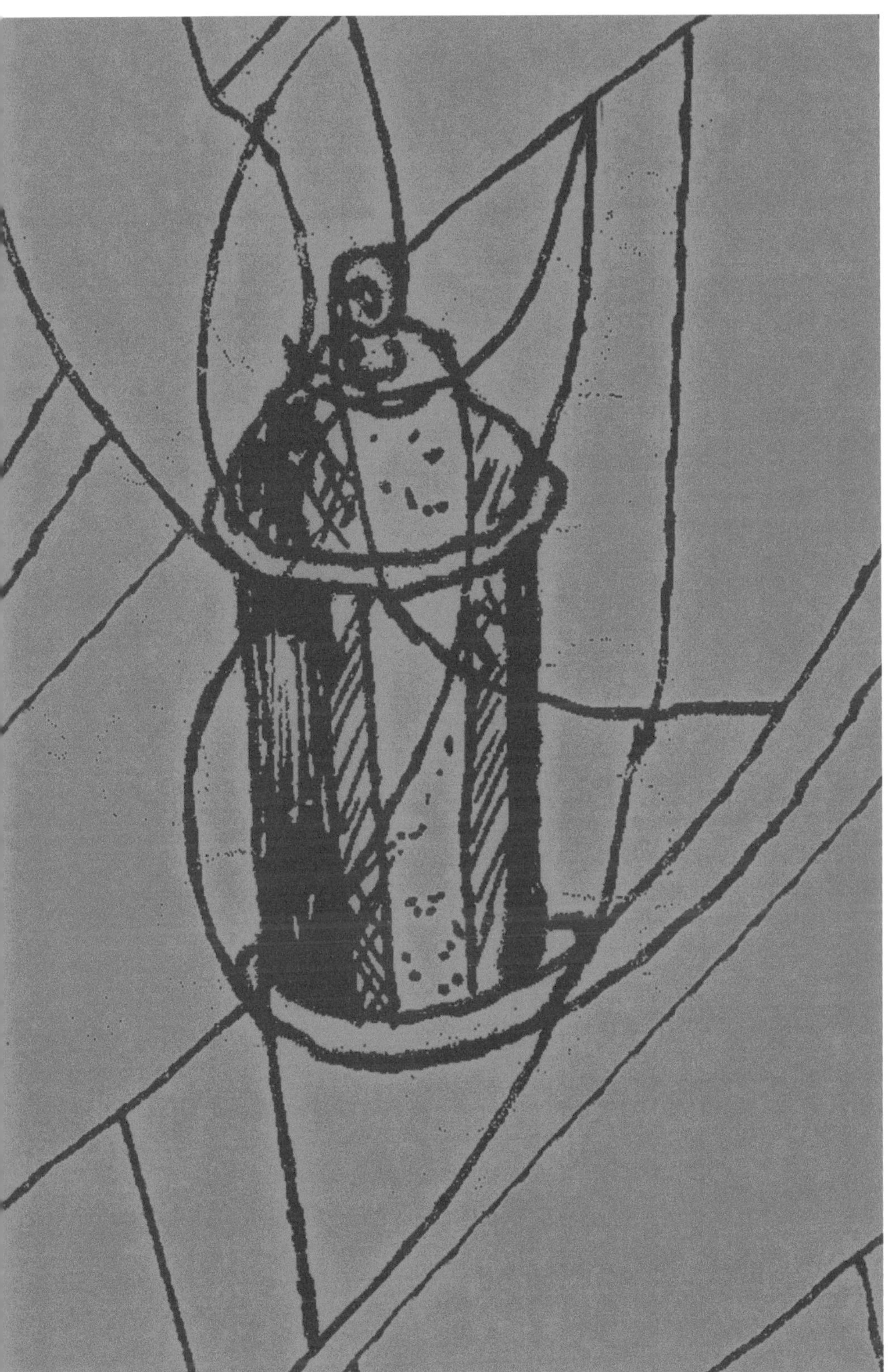

"Alieno"
2021
Digital

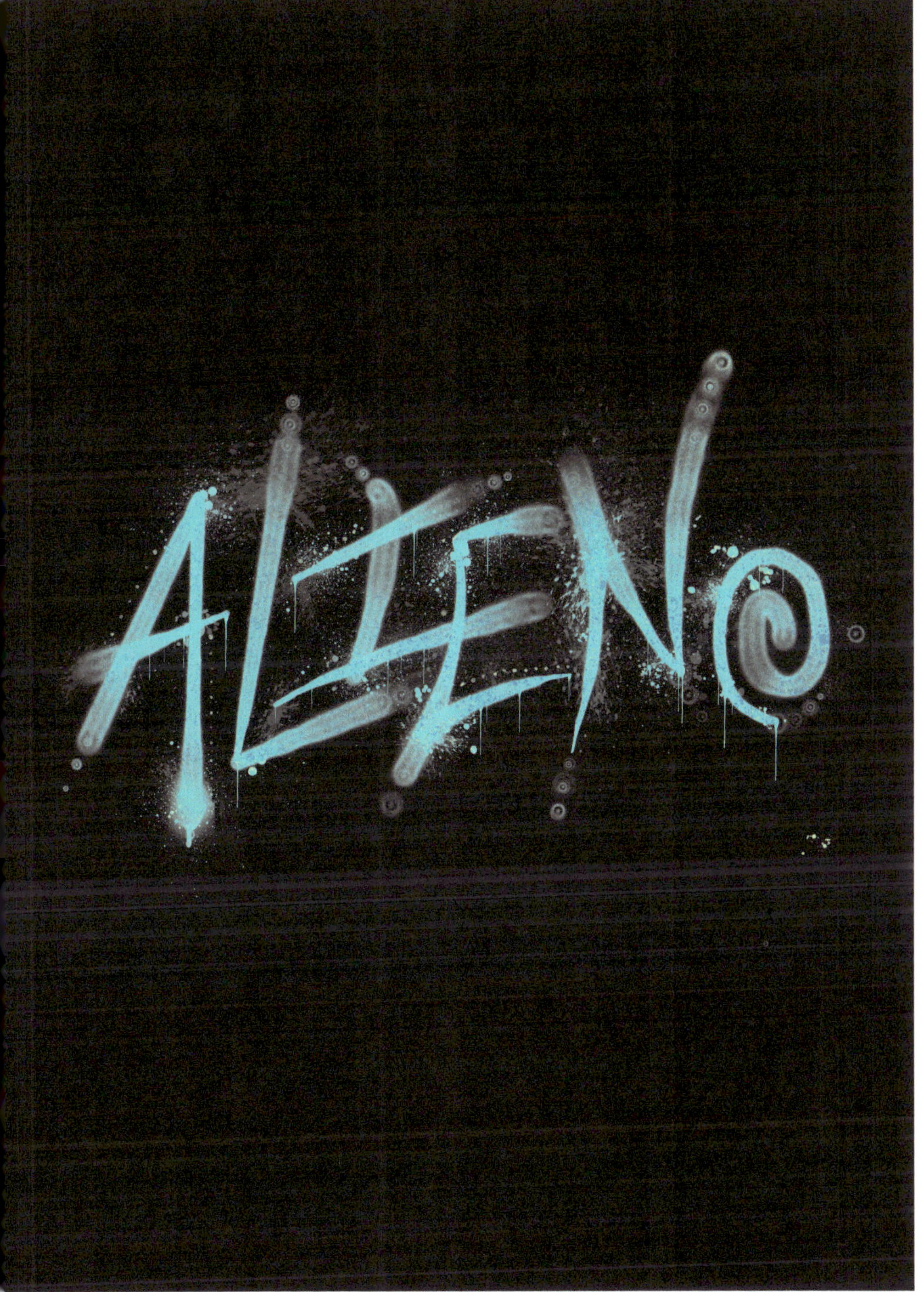

ALIENO

"Mermaid Grafitti"
2021
Digital Illustration

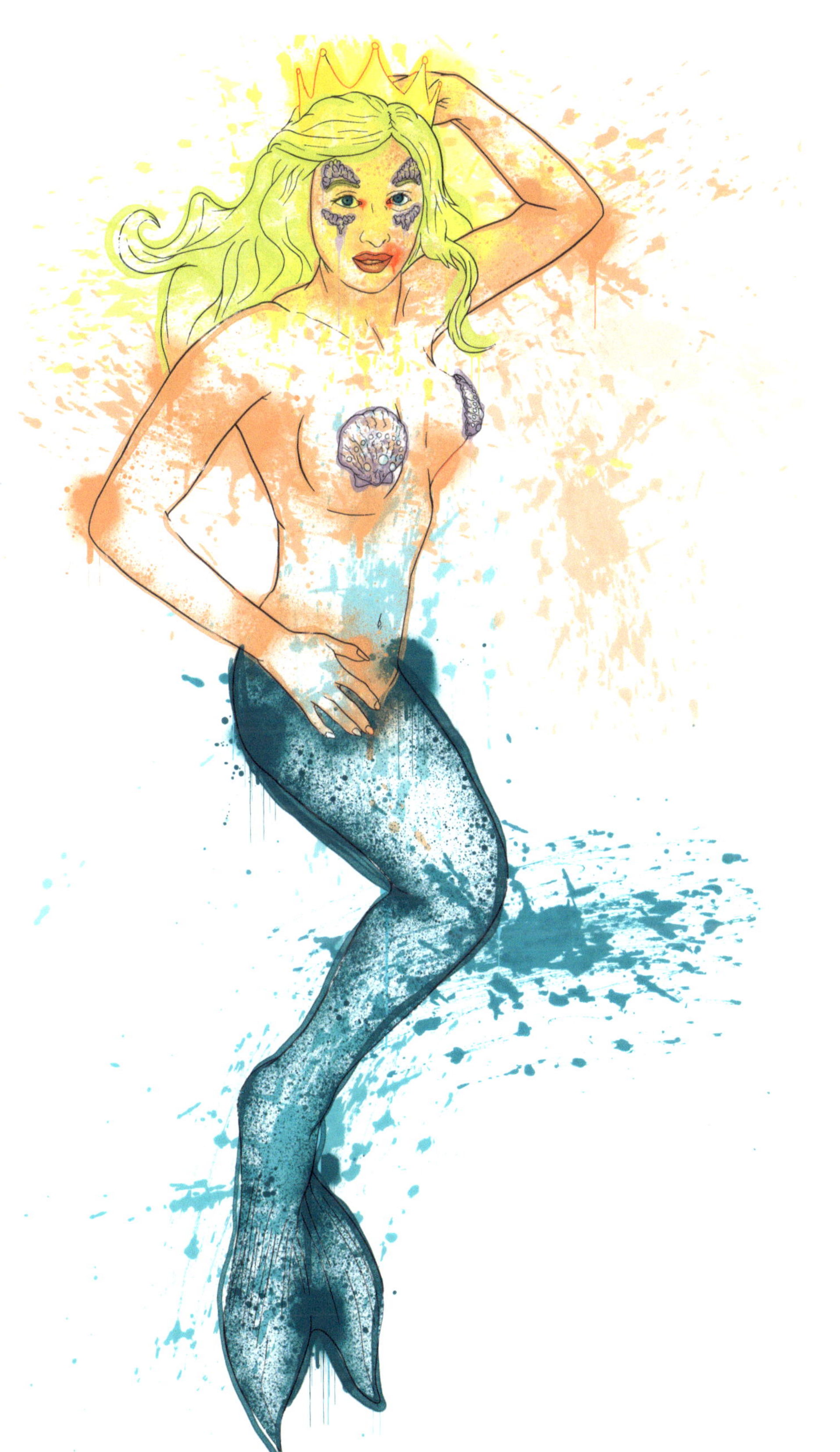

"White Guitar from Heaven"
2023
Custom Guitar and Photo Manipulation

"Tree Guitar from Space"
2023
Custom Guitar and Photo Manipulation

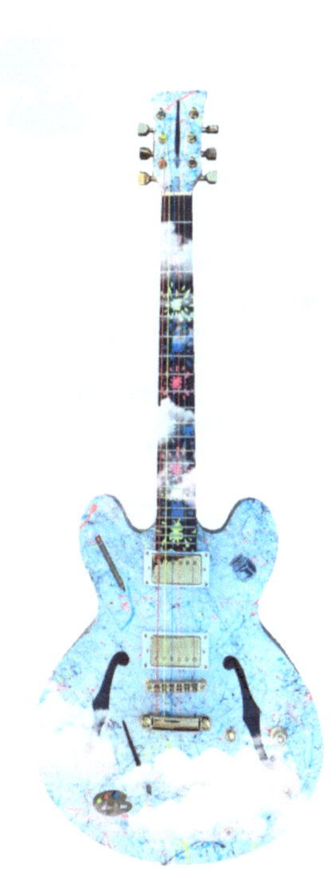
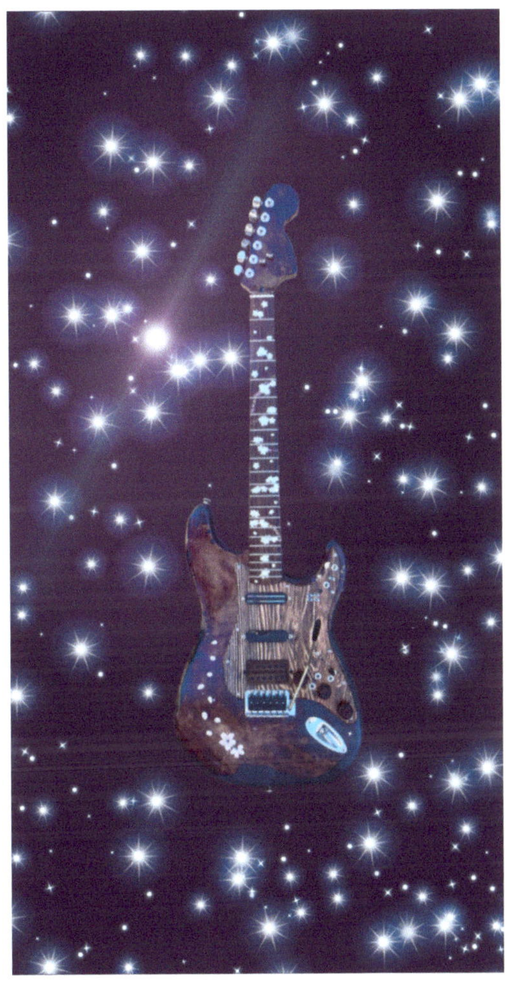

"Space Lines"
2022
Digital Illustration

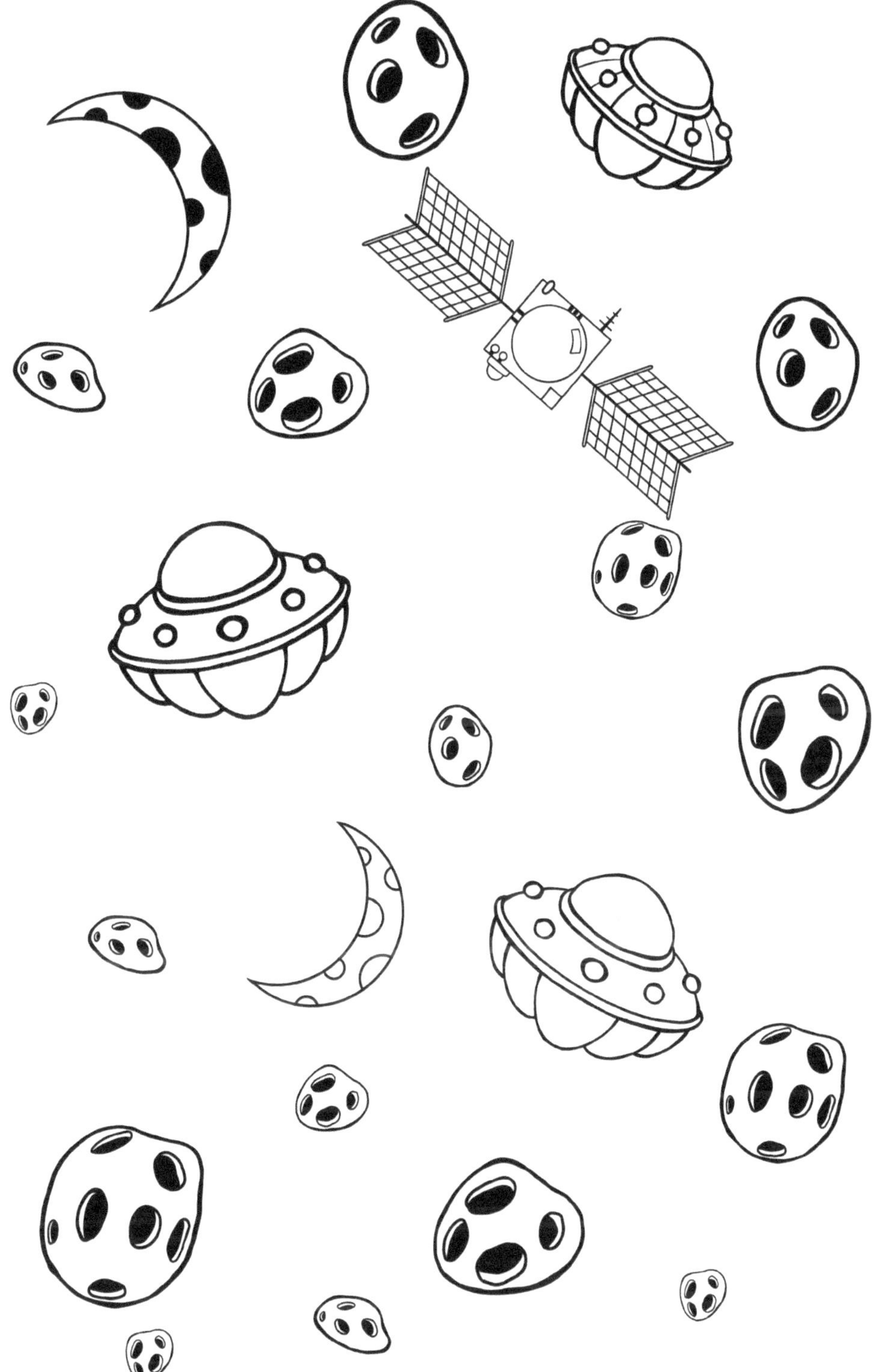

"Wooden Guitar"
2022
Digital

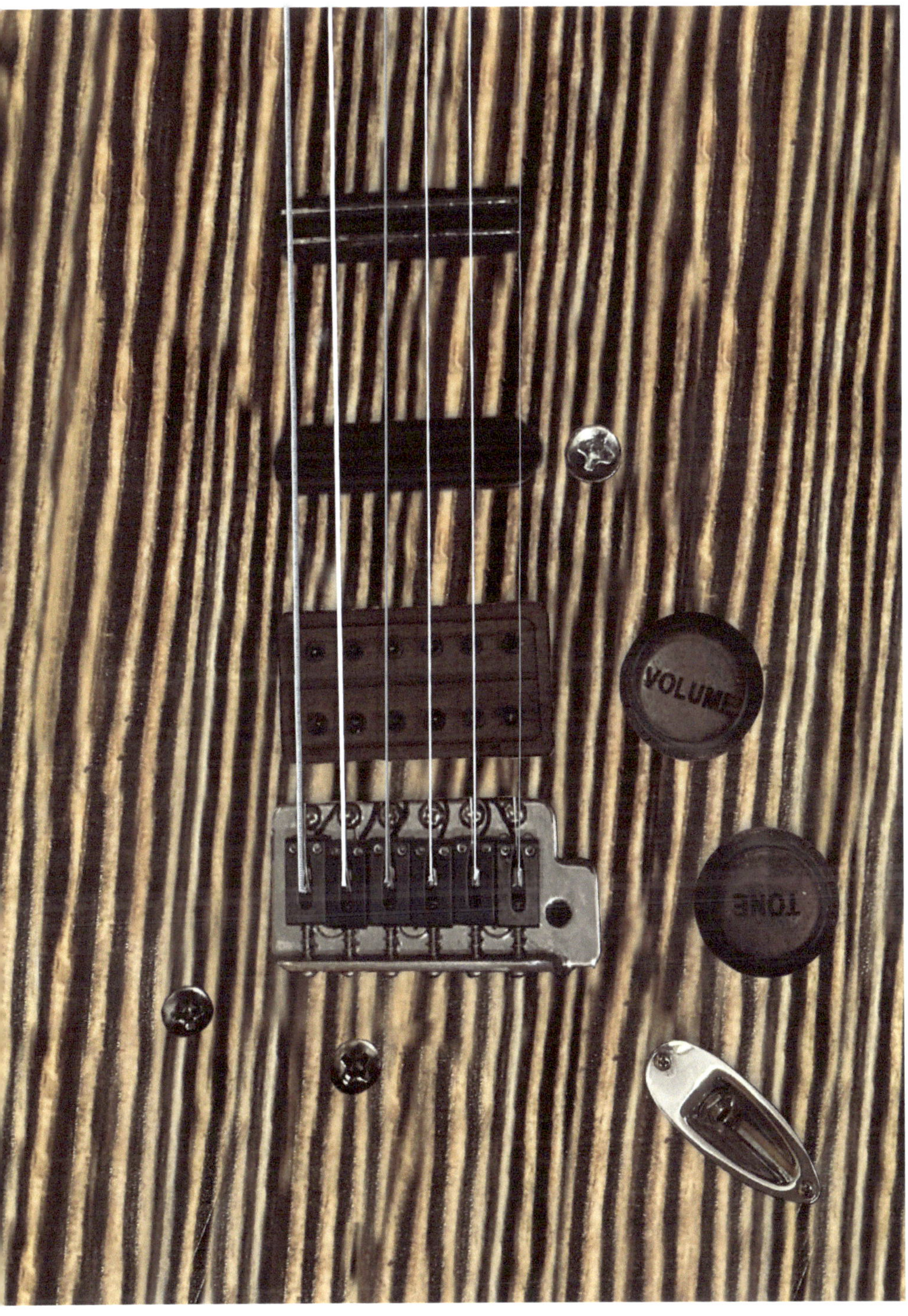

VOLUME
TONE

"Pixel Pianos"
2020
Digital Music Visualizer & Pixel

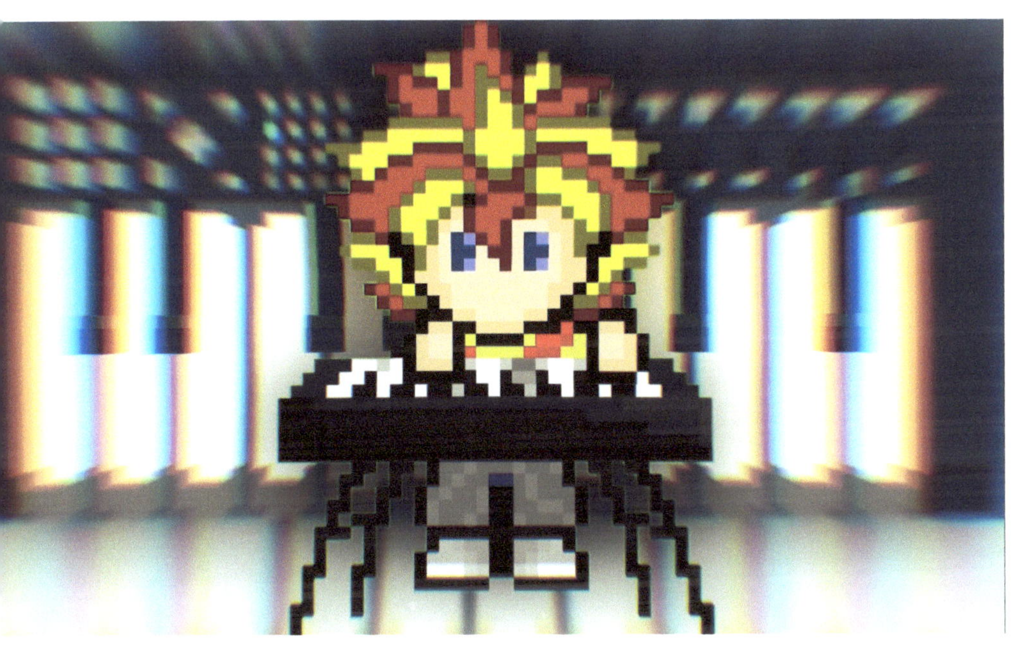

"Hamster Harmonica"
2023
Digital, Graphite & Music Visualizer

"Emo Alien Banjo #1"
2023
Digital, Graphite & Music Visualizer

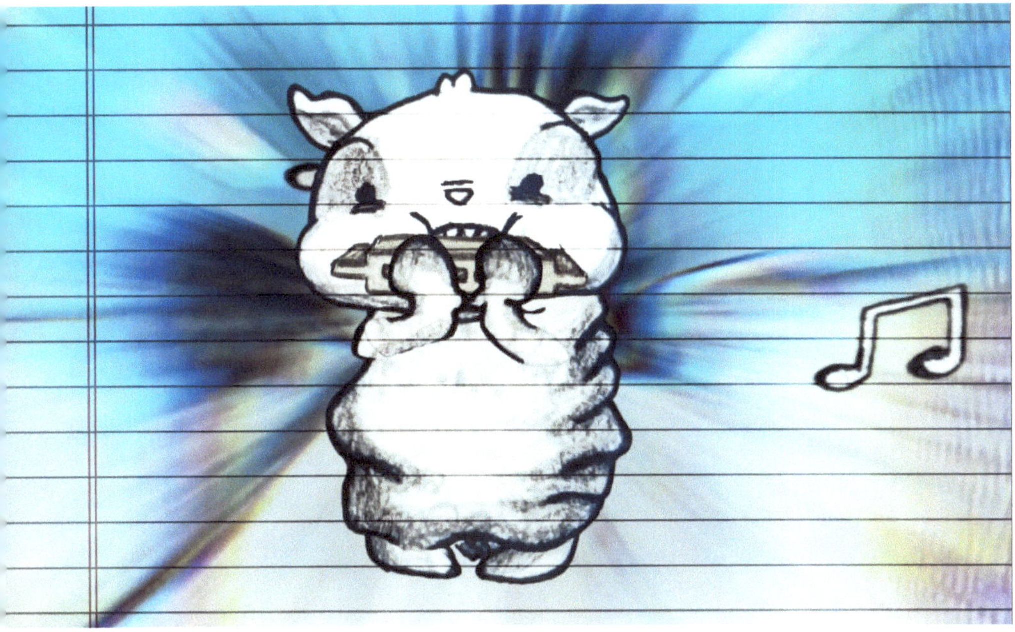

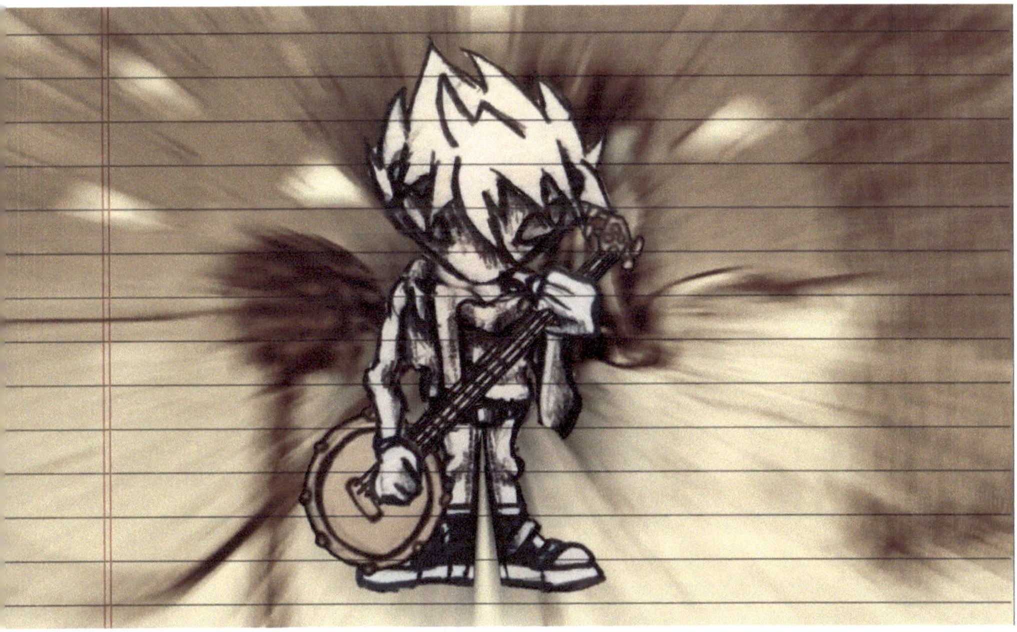

"Emo Alien Banjo #2"
2023
Digital, Graphite & Music Visualizer

"Hamster Cigar Box"
2023
Digital, Graphite & Music Visualizer

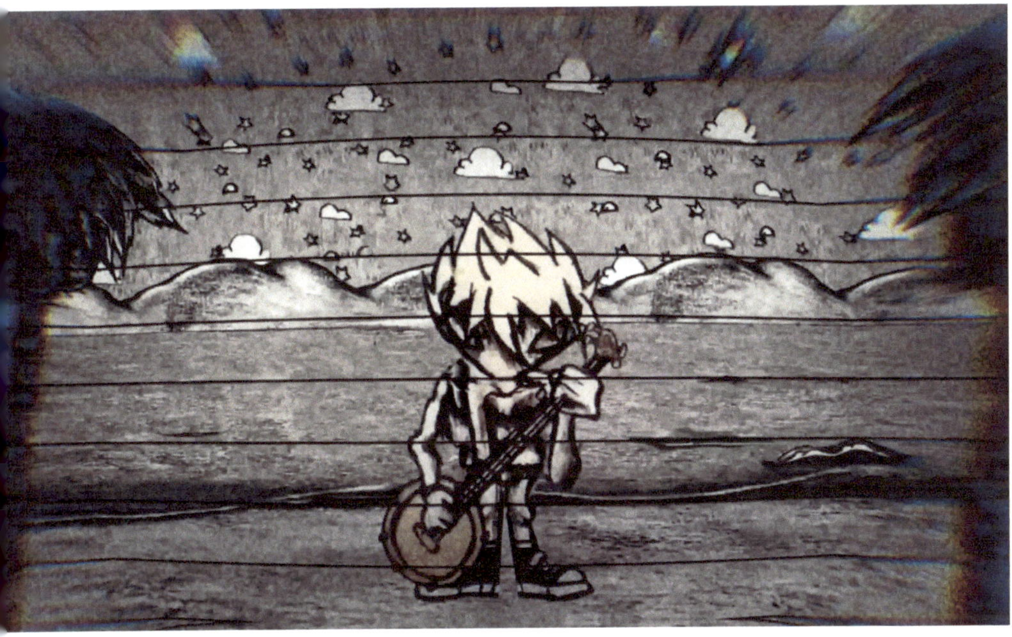

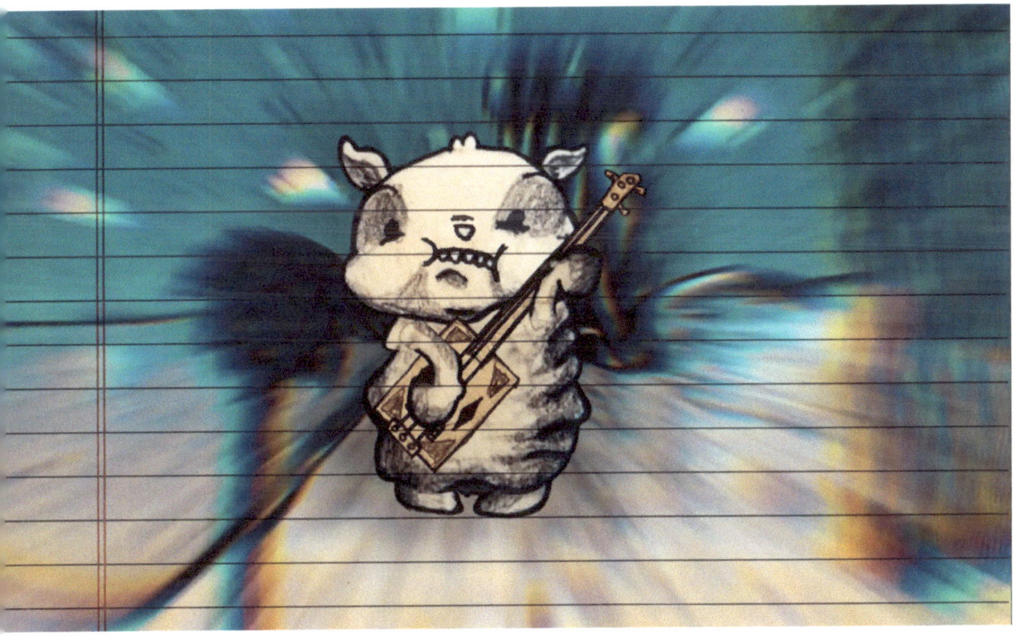

"Kingdom Kitty"
2018
Digital & Graphite

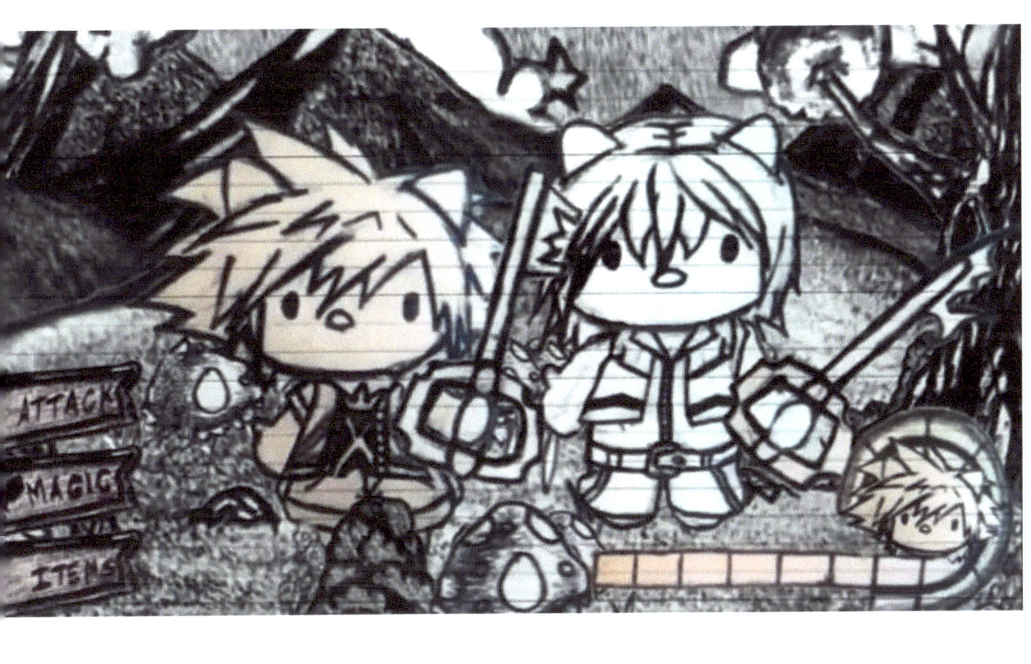
ATTACK
MAGIC
ITEMS

"Divinity Website #1"
2010
Web Design

"Divinity Website #2"
2010
Web Design

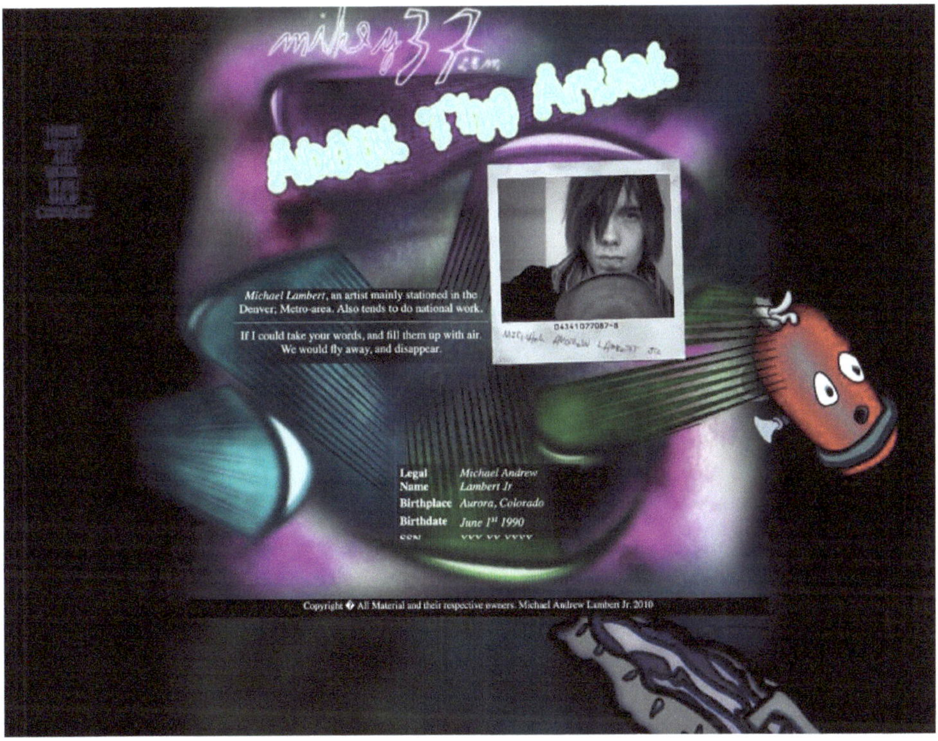

mikey37
About The Artist

Michael Lambert, an artist mainly stationed in the Denver; Metro-area. Also tends to do national work.

If I could take your words, and fill them up with air. We would fly away, and disappear.

04341077087-8
MICHAEL ANDREW LAMBERT JR

Legal Name   Michael Andrew Lambert Jr
Birthplace   Aurora, Colorado
Birthdate   June 1st 1990
SSN   XXX-XX-XXXX

Copyright © All Material and their respective owners. Michael Andrew Lambert Jr. 2010

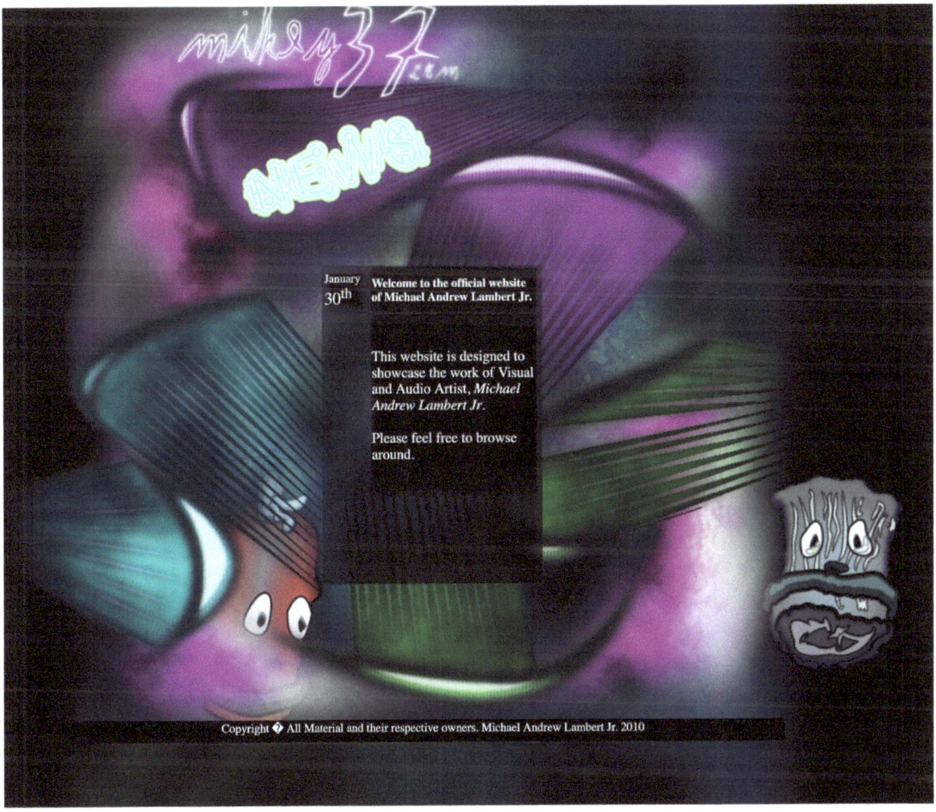

mikey37
NEWS

January 30th

Welcome to the official website of Michael Andrew Lambert Jr.

This website is designed to showcase the work of Visual and Audio Artist, Michael Andrew Lambert Jr.

Please feel free to browse around.

Copyright © All Material and their respective owners. Michael Andrew Lambert Jr. 2010

"DeadSexyMikey Myspace Design"
2009
Web Design

"Blue and Yellow"
2010
Web Design

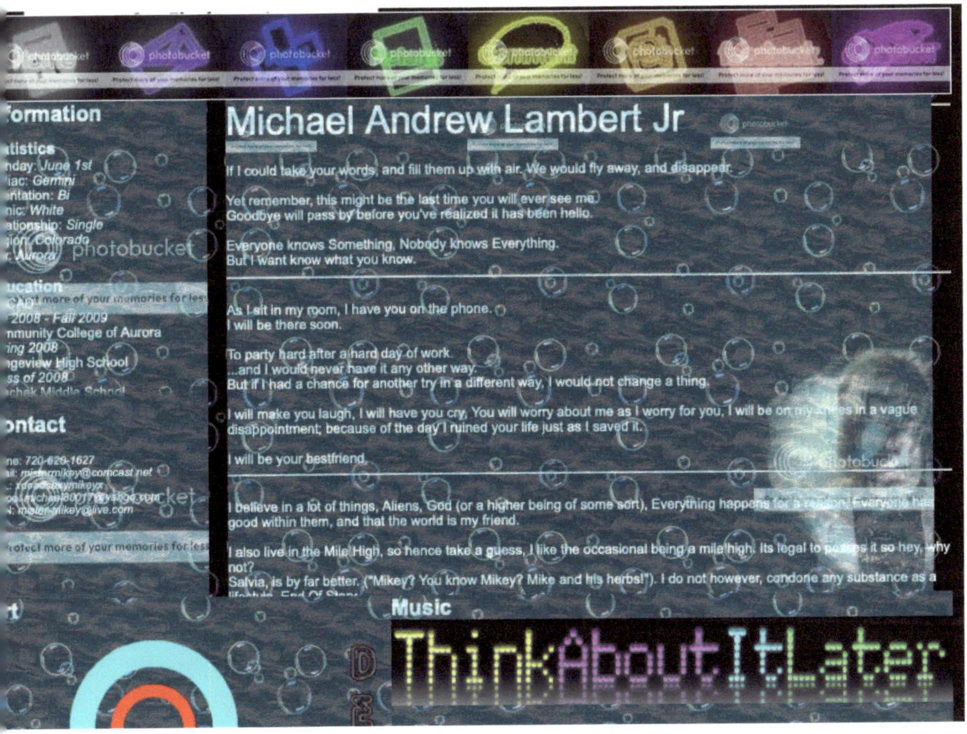

Michael Andrew Lambert Jr

formation

tistics
nday: *June 1st*
iac: *Gemini*
ntation: *Bi*
nic: *White*
ationship: *Single*
ion: *Colorado*
: *Aurora*

ucation
... 2008 - Fall 2009
mmunity College of Aurora
ing 2008
ngeview High School
ss of 2008
chak Middle School

ontact
ne: 720-629-1627
il: mistrmikey@comcast.net
: xdeadboxymikeyx
oo: michael180017@yahoo.com
: mister-mikey@live.com

If I could take your words, and fill them up with air. We would fly away, and disappear.

Yet remember, this might be the last time you will ever see me.
Goodbye will pass by before you've realized it has been hello.

Everyone knows Something, Nobody knows Everything.
But I want know what you know.

As I sit in my room, I have you on the phone.
I will be there soon.

To party hard after a hard day of work.
...and I would never have it any other way.
But if I had a chance for another try in a different way, I would not change a thing.

I will make you laugh, I will have you cry, You will worry about me as I worry for you, I will be on my knees in a vague disappointment; because of the day I ruined your life just as I saved it.

I will be your bestfriend.

I believe in a lot of things, Aliens, God (or a higher being of some sort), Everything happens for a reason, Everyone has good within them, and that the world is my friend.

I also live in the Mile High, so hence take a guess, I like the occasional being a mile high. Its legal to possess it so hey, why not?
Salvia, is by far better. ("Mikey? You know Mikey? Mike and his herbs!"). I do not however, condone any substance as a lifestyle. End Of Story.

Music

ThinkAboutItLater

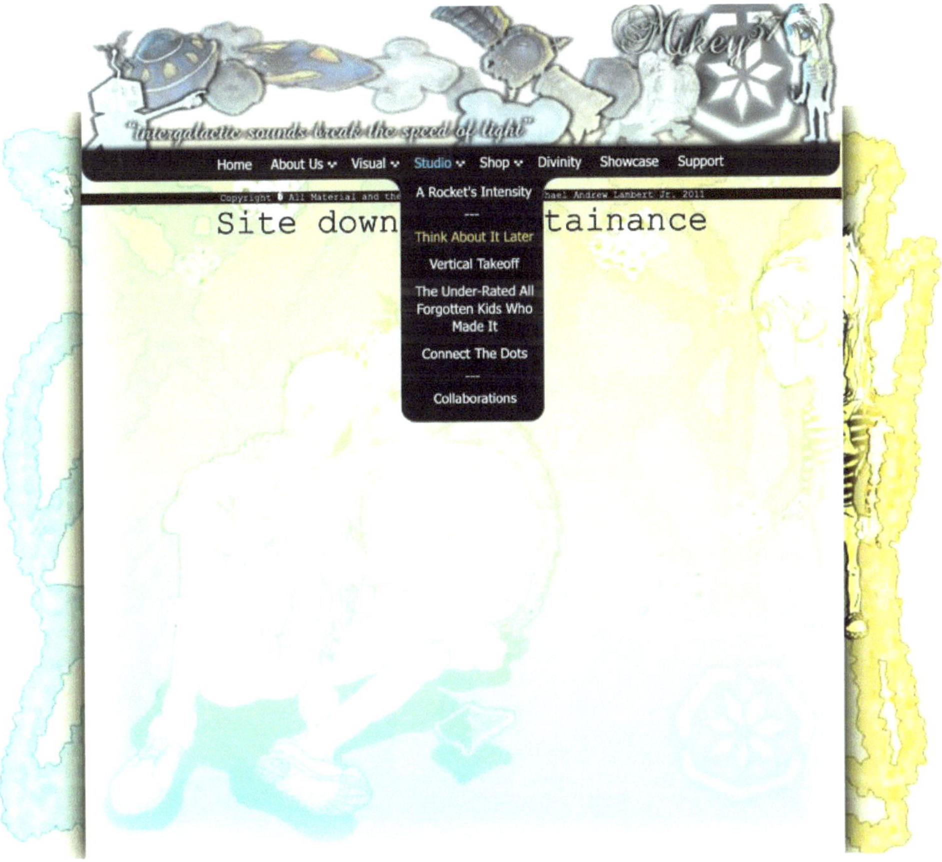

Mikey

"intergalactic sounds break the speed of light"

Home About Us ⌄ Visual ⌄ Studio ⌄ Shop ⌄ Divinity Showcase Support

Site down for maintainance

A Rocket's Intensity

Think About It Later

Vertical Takeoff

The Under-Rated All Forgotten Kids Who Made It

Connect The Dots

Collaborations

"AR3NA Gameboy #1"
2023
Gameboy Game

"AR3NA Gameboy #1"
2023
Gameboy Game

"AR3NA Gameboy #1"
2023
Gameboy Game

"AR3NA #NES"
2024
NES Game

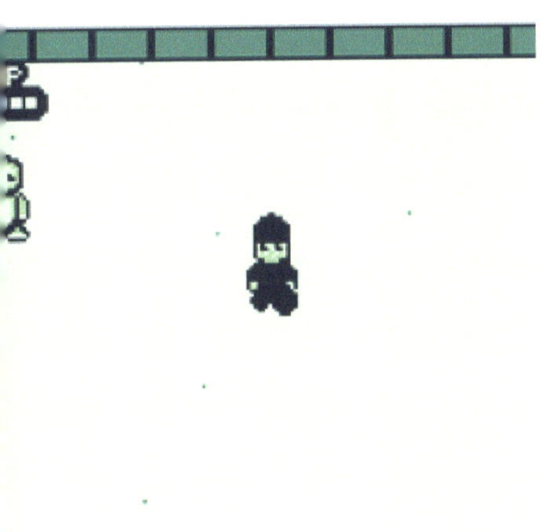

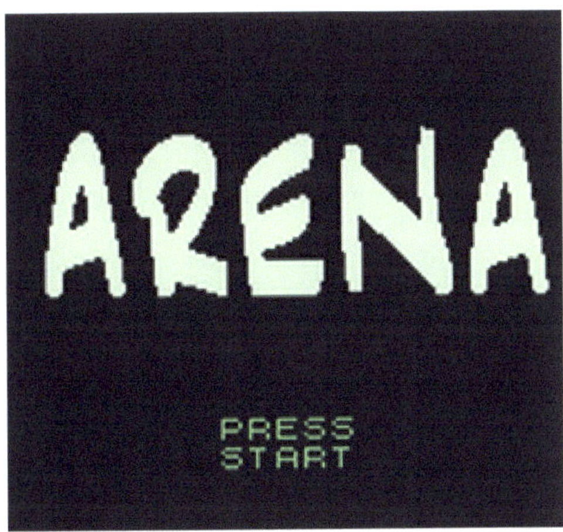

ARENA
PRESS
START

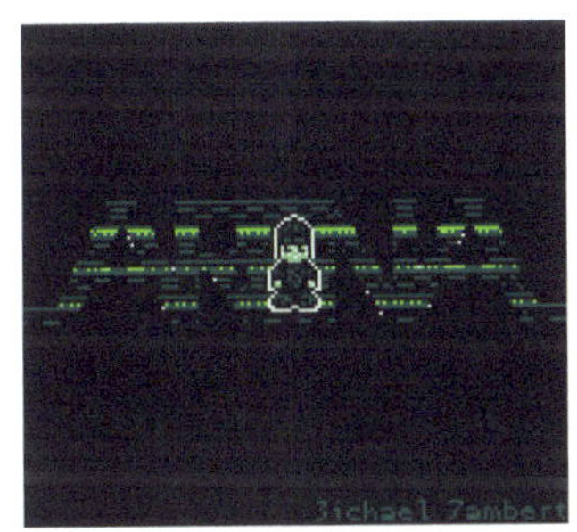

Michael Zambert

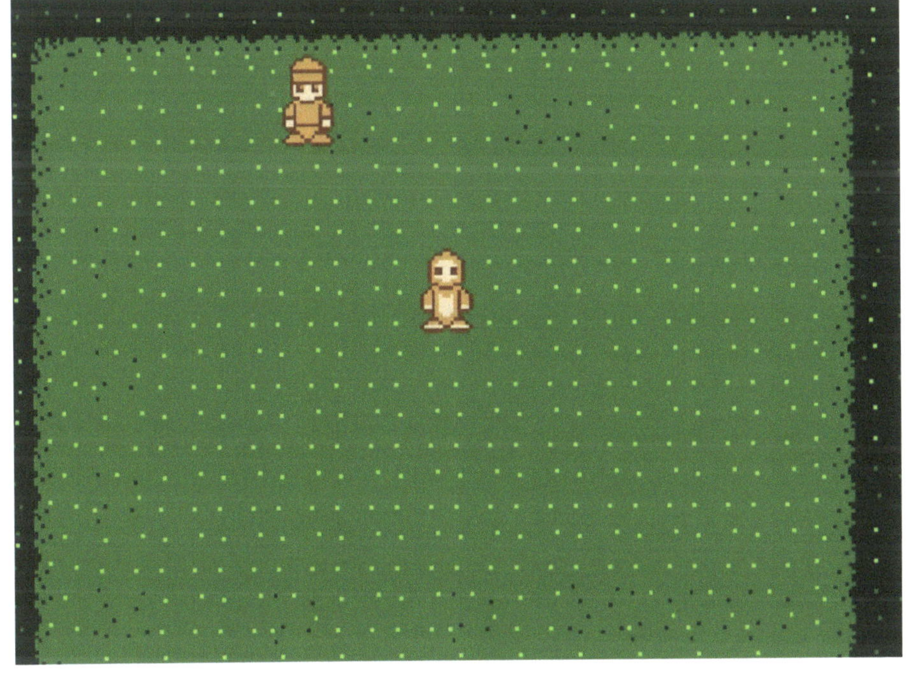

"Sand Dunes"
2022
Digital Illustration

"Oceana"
2022
Digital Illustration

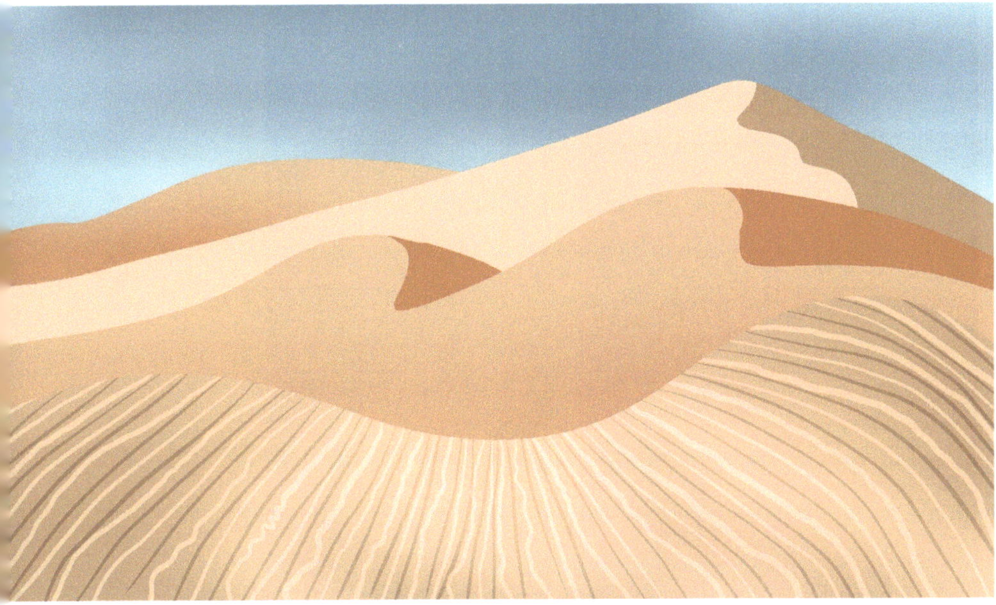

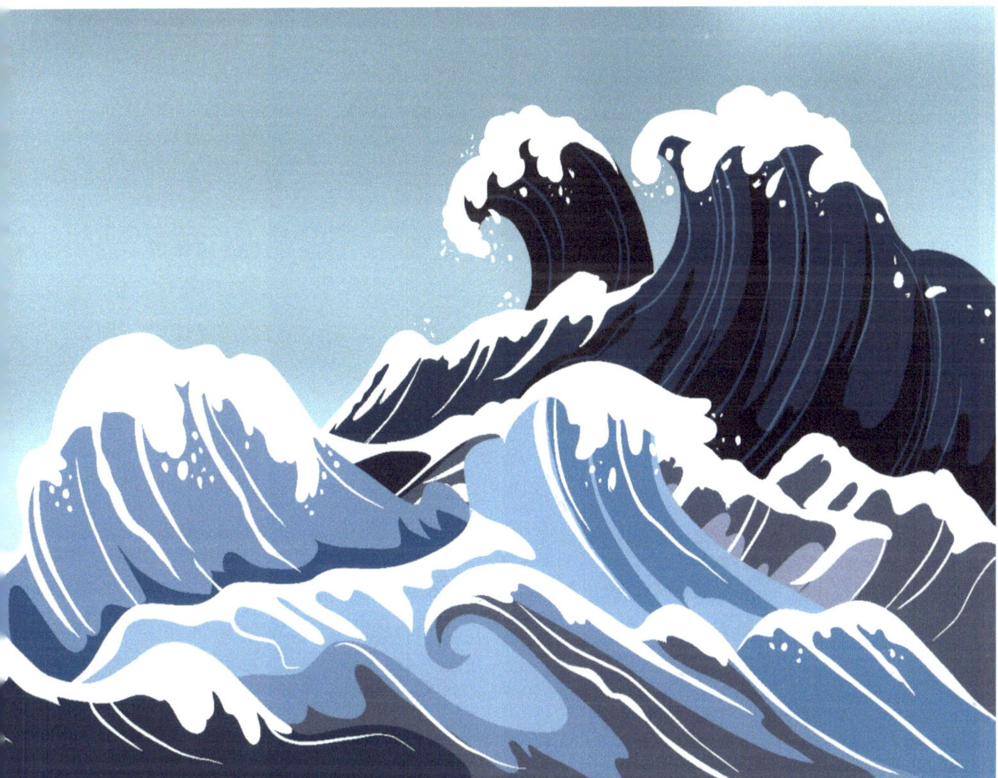

"Skyline"
2022
Digital Illustration

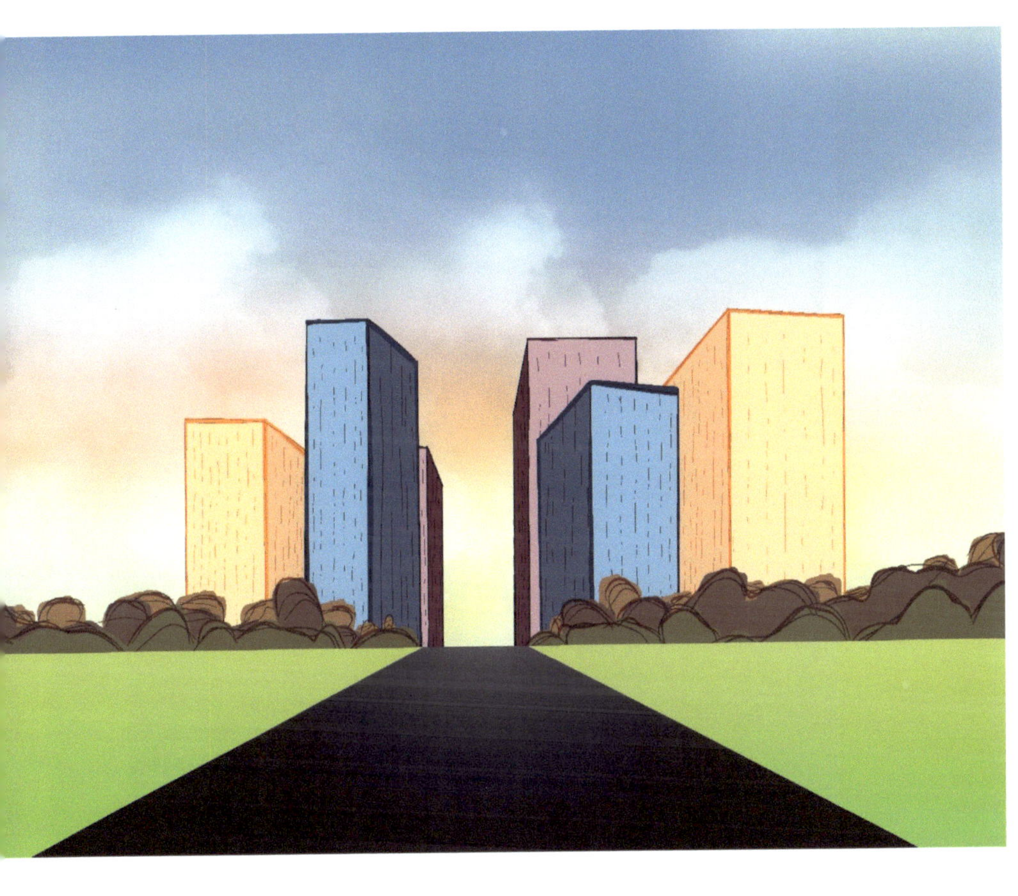

"Bonnie"
2024
Digital Illustration & Charcoal

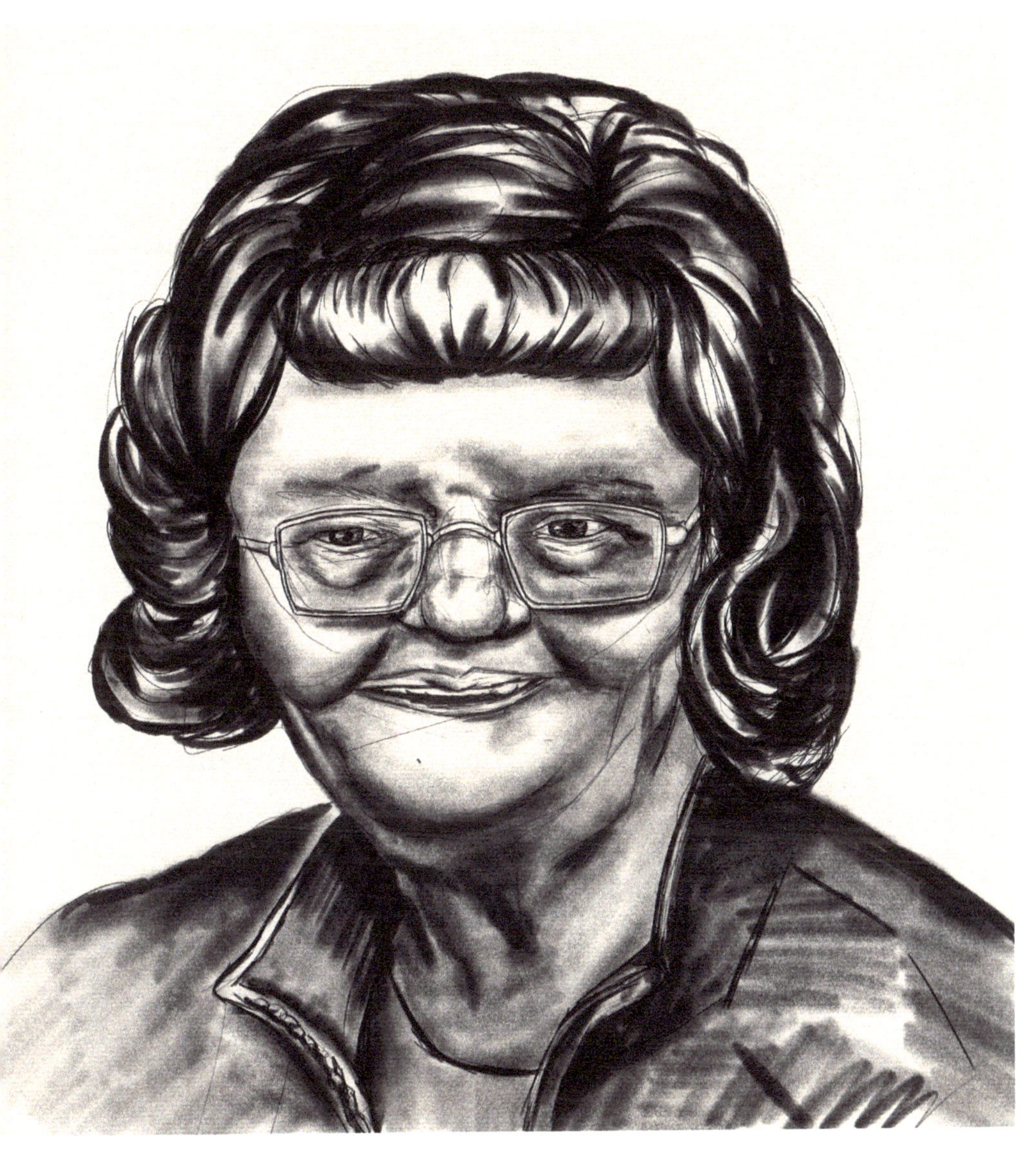

"Rappette"
2018
Digital Illustration

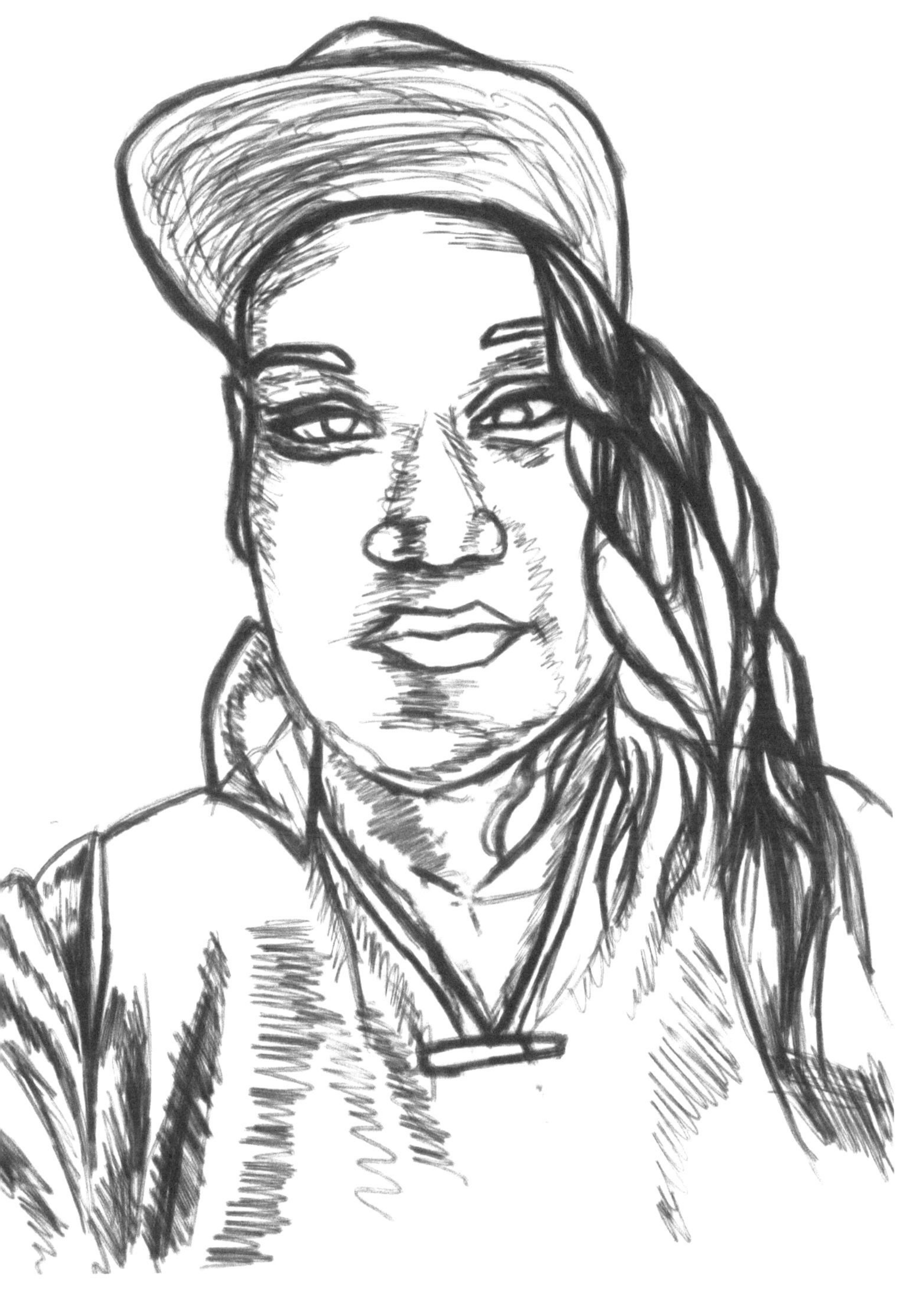

"Him & Her"
2018
Digital Illustration

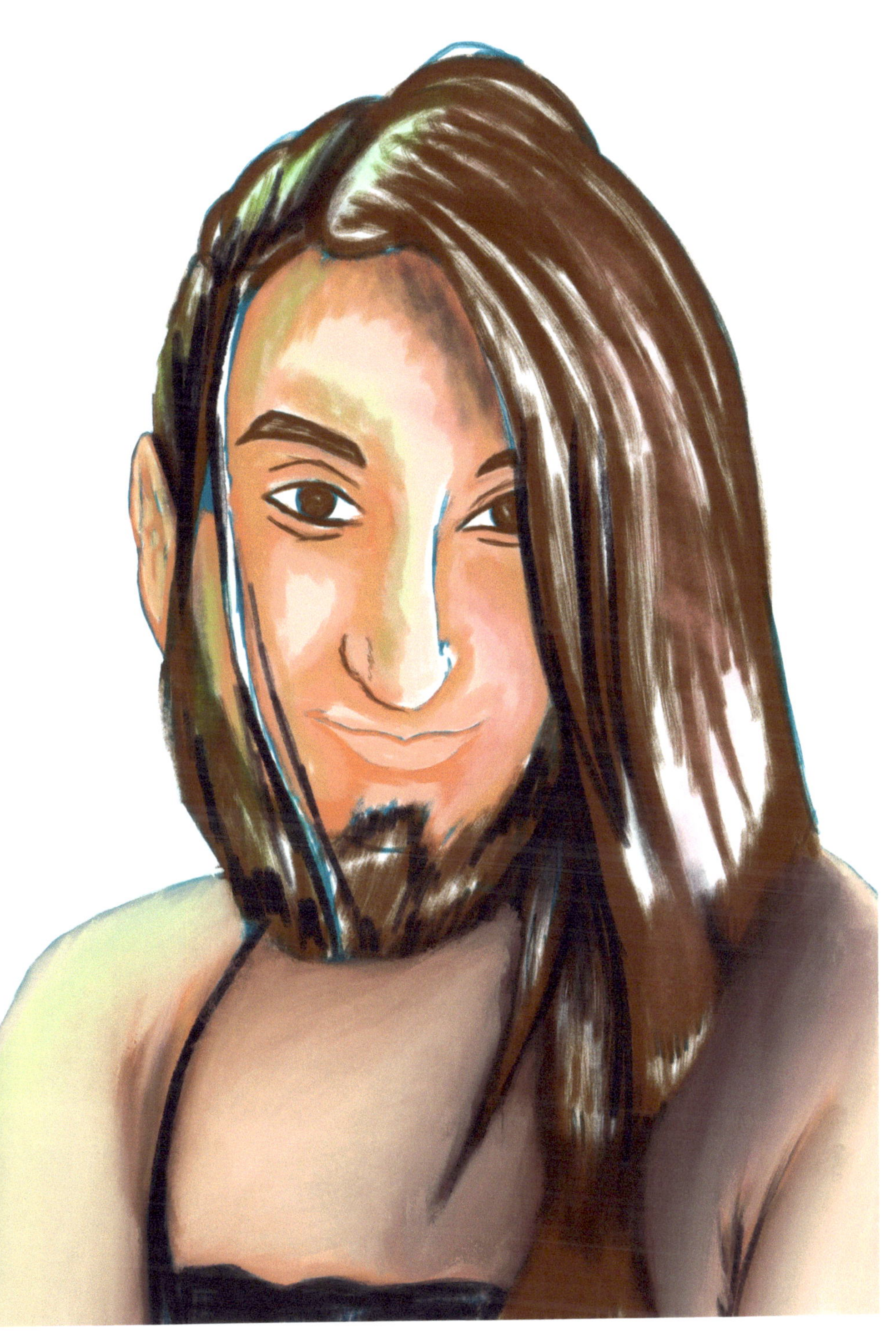

"Gaze"
2021
Digital Illustration

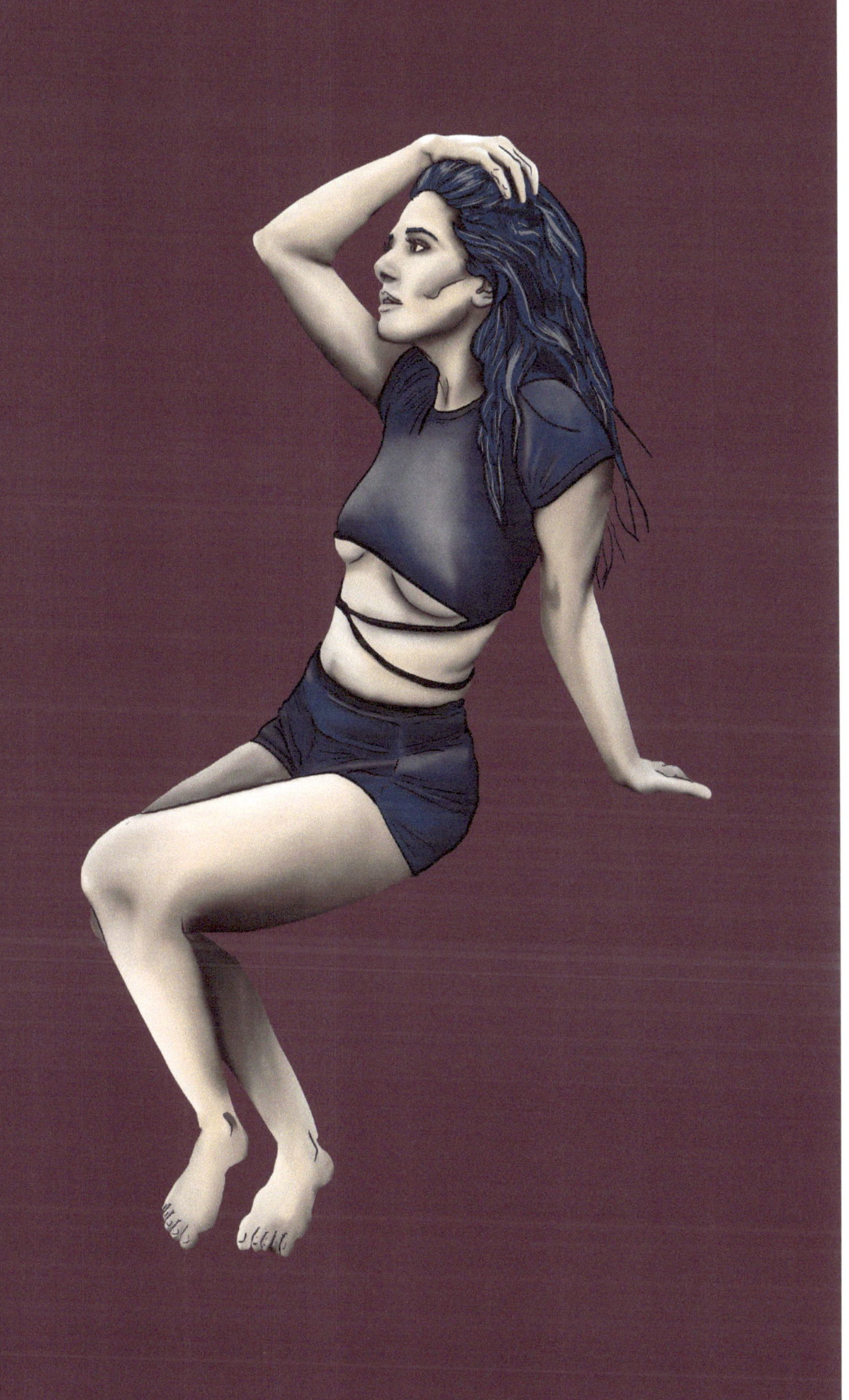

"Tree"
2020
Digital Illustration

"Cactus"
2020
Digital Illustration

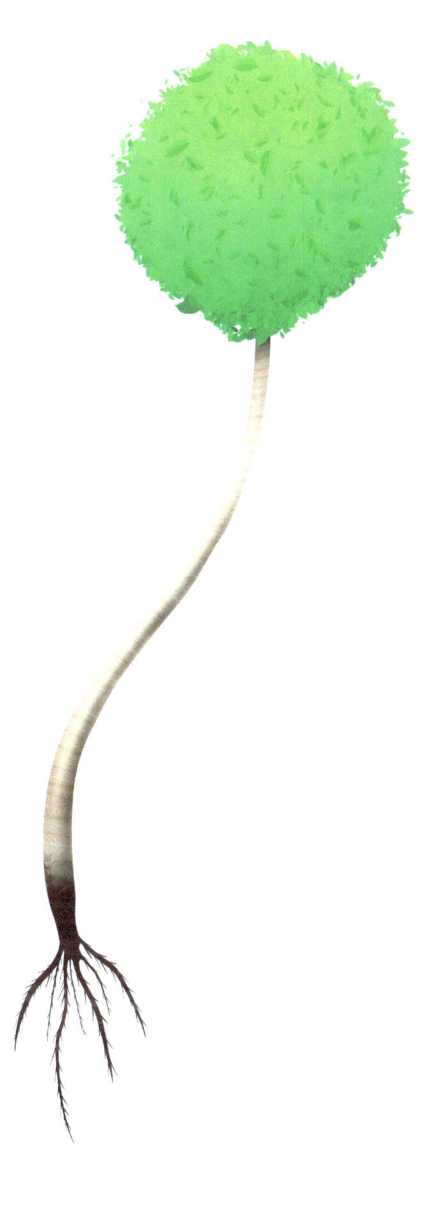
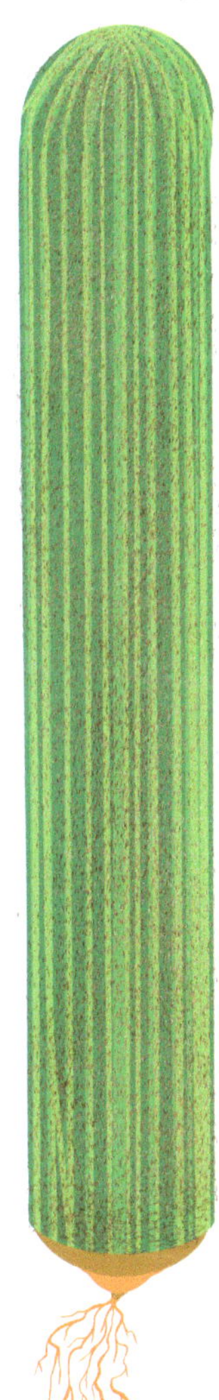

"Xero"
2019
Digital Illustration & Character Design

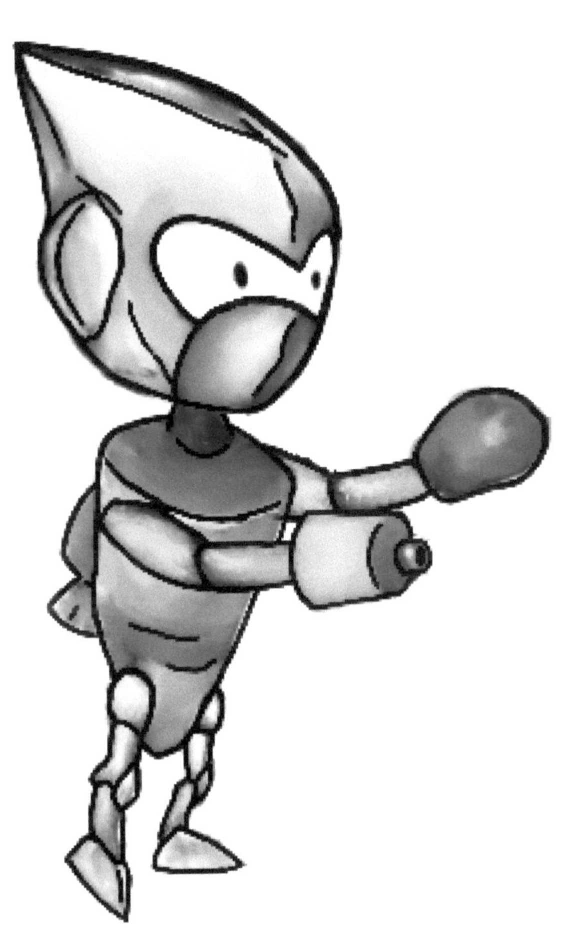

"Pylon"
2012
Photography

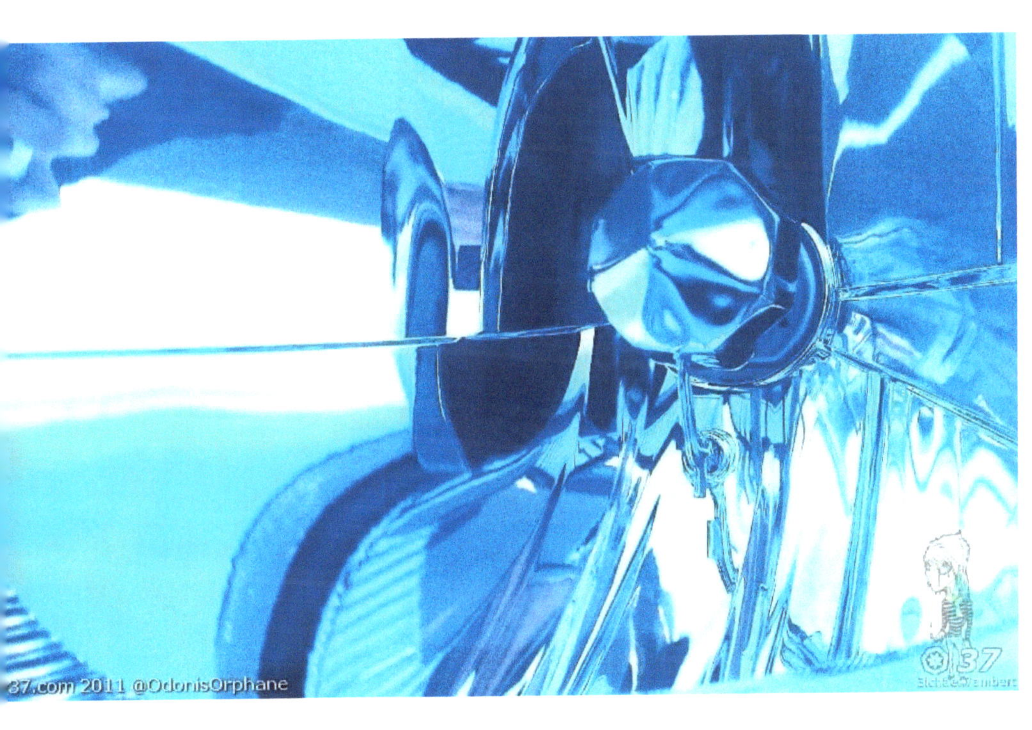
37.com 2011 @OdonisOrphane
37

"Odonis Snowboarding"
2018
Digital Illustration

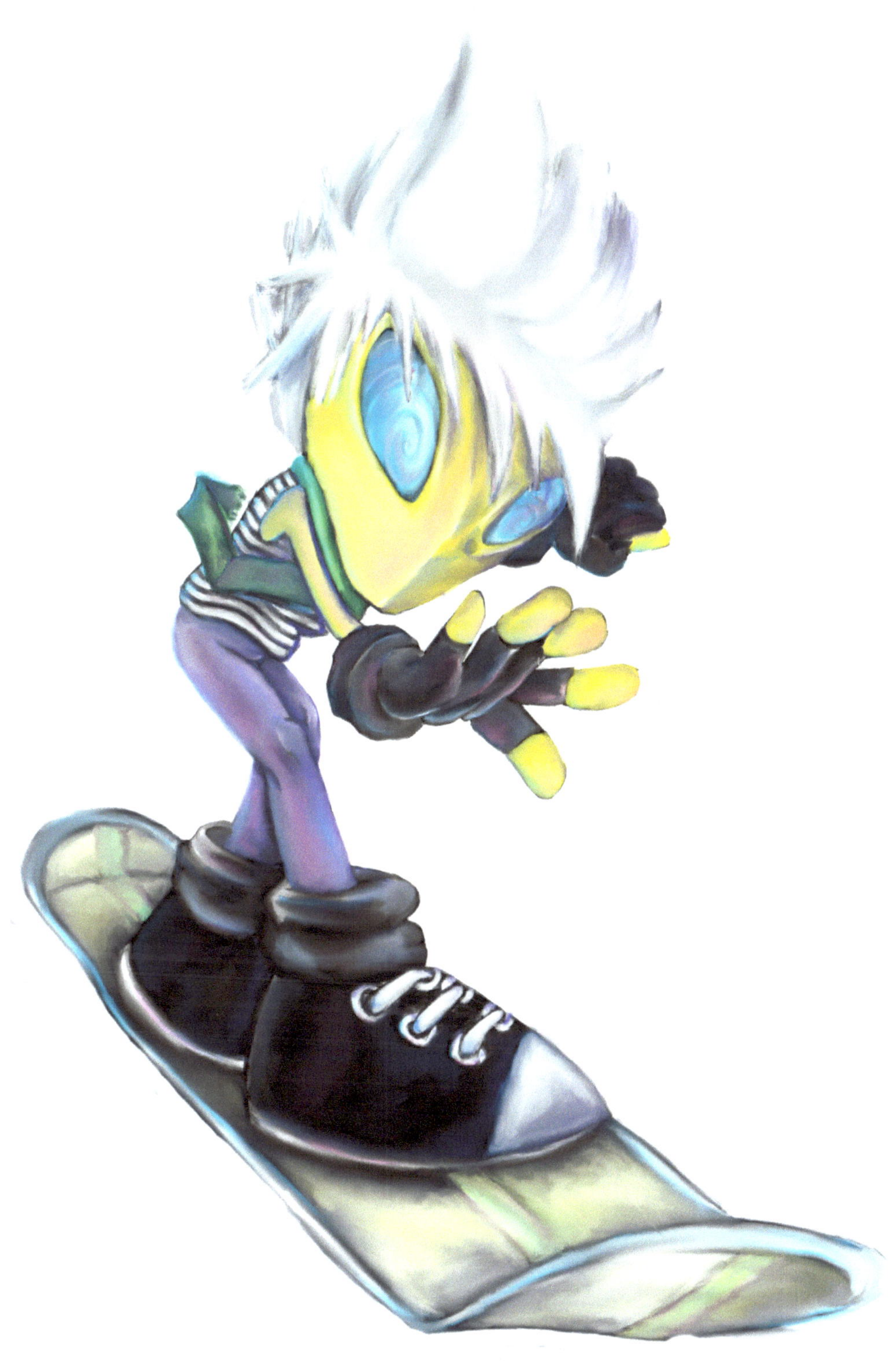

"Guitar Jesus"
2023
Digital, Model & Photography

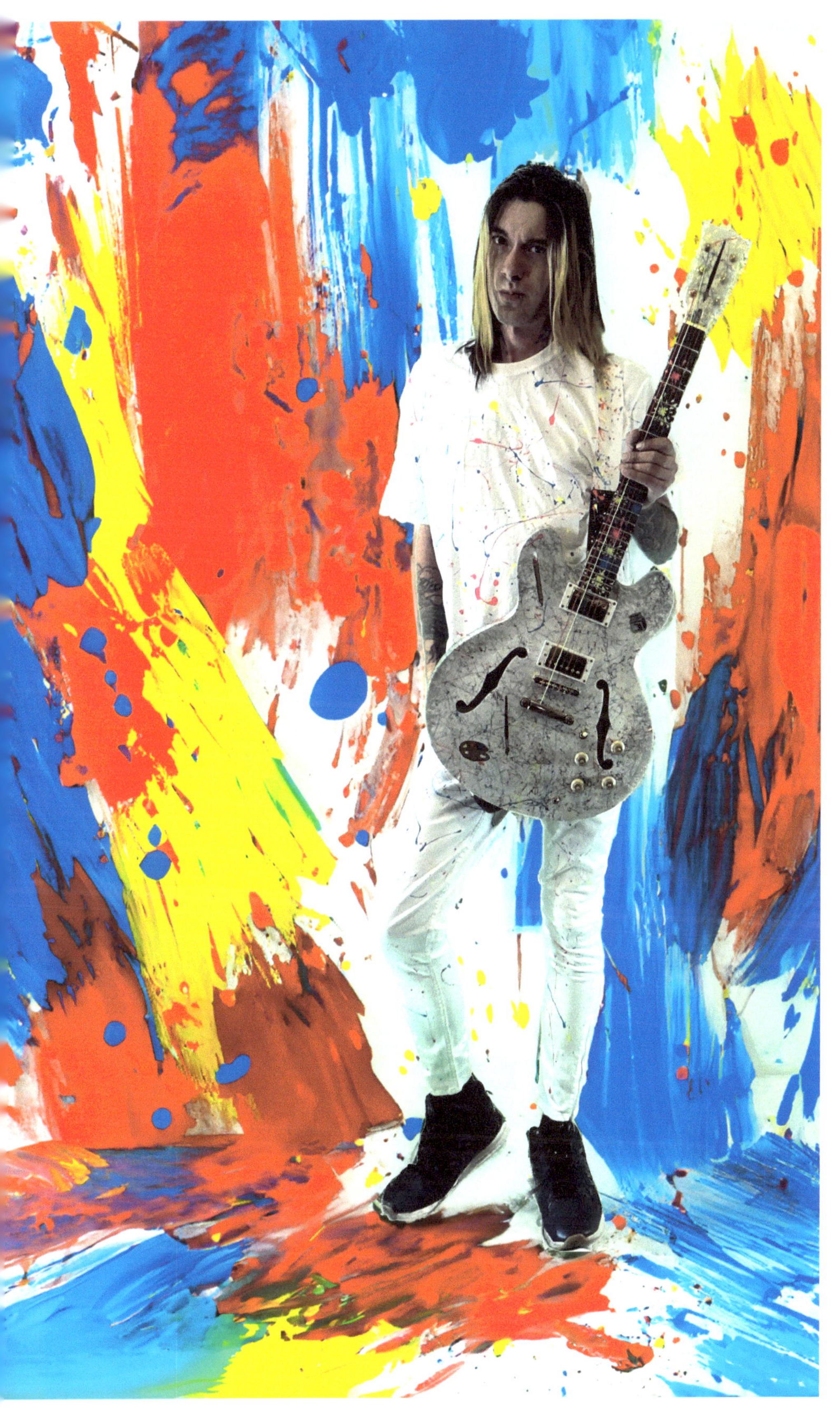

"Pixel Pianist"
2022
Pixel

"Pixel Plano"
2022
Pixel

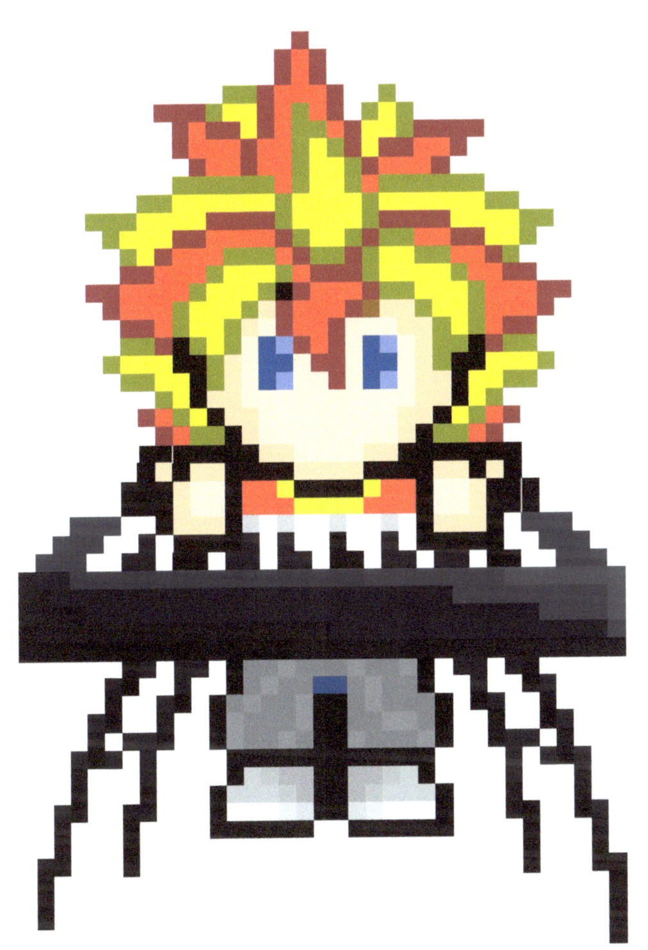

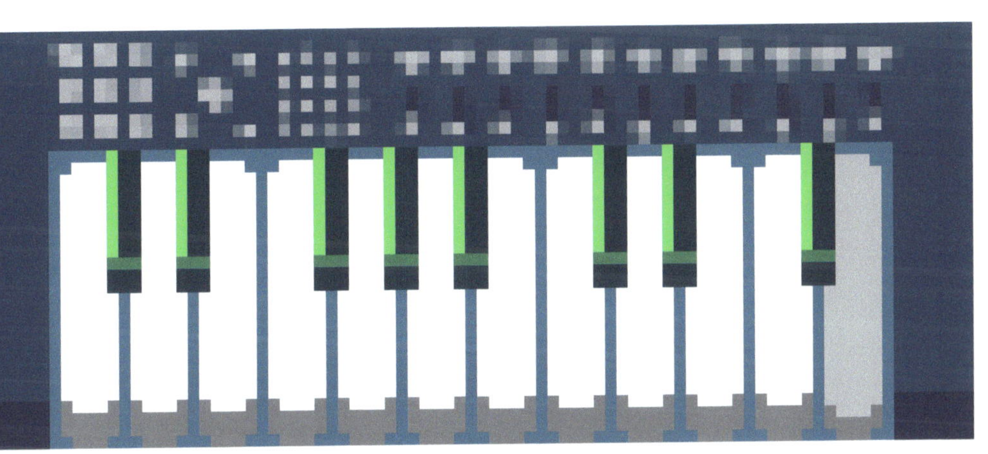

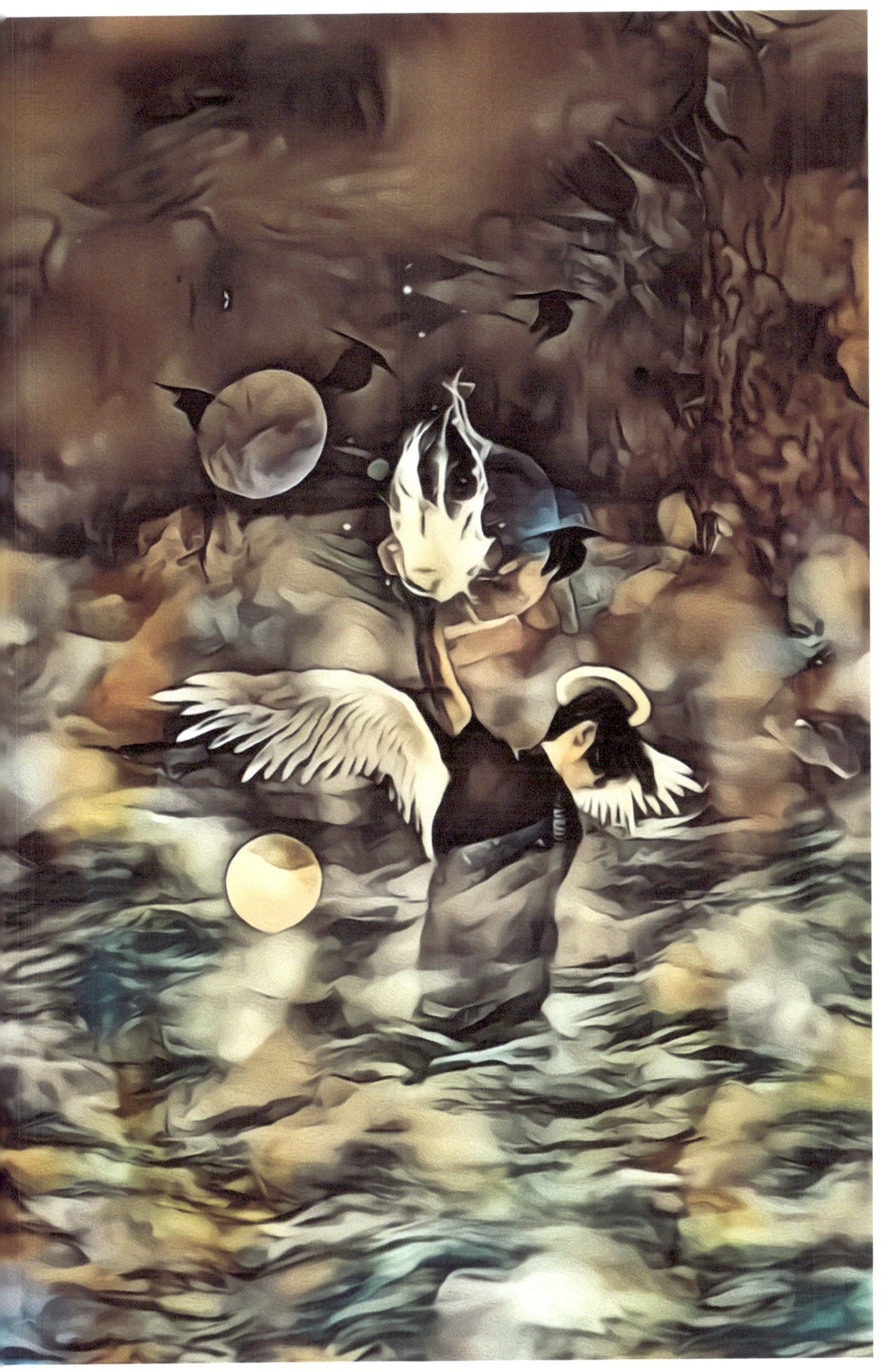